Sunk by Stukas, Survived at Salerno

Sunk by Stukas, Survived at Salerno

The Memoirs of
Captain Tony McCrum RN (Rtd)

Pen & Sword
MARITIME

First published in Great Britain in 2010 by
Pen & Sword Maritime
an imprint of
Pen & Sword Books Ltd
47 Church Street
Barnsley
South Yorkshire
S70 2AS

Copyright © Tony McCrum 2010

ISBN 978-1-84884-251-9

A CIP catalogue record for this book is available from the British Library.

Typeset in 11pt Ehrhardt by
Mac Style, Beverley, E. Yorkshire

Printed and bound in the UK by CPI

Pen & Sword Books Ltd incorporates the imprints of Pen & Sword
Aviation, Pen & Sword Maritime, Pen & Sword Military, Wharncliffe
Local History, Pen and Sword Select, Pen and Sword Military Classics and
Leo Cooper.

For a complete list of Pen & Sword titles please contact
PEN & SWORD BOOKS LIMITED
47 Church Street, Barnsley, South Yorkshire, S70 2AS, England
E-mail: enquiries@pen-and-sword.co.uk
Website: www.pen-and-sword.co.uk

Contents

Dedication

For Liz

But when the blast of war blows in our ears
Then imitate the action of the tiger;
Stiffen the sinews, summon up the blood
Disguise fair nature with hard favoured rage;
Then lend the eye a terrible aspect.

(Shakespeare, Henry V)

Chapter One

Conditioning

The Royal Naval College, Dartmouth 1932–1936

For me, World War II started on Armistice Day, 11 November 1918. I was born in March 1919 while my mother was recovering from the Spanish flu pandemic, which killed 40 million worldwide and nearly killed her and me. I grew up under the horrors of the Great War, as it was called. As a schoolboy I studied the history of that ghastly struggle. I read how on the first day of the Battle of the Somme in France (1916) there were 60,000 British casualties and how in the even more terrible Passchendaele campaign (August to September 1917) there were 300,000 dead and wounded, many of them drowned in the mud of Flanders fields.

At the Royal Naval College at Dartmouth I read widely amongst the war poets and the anti-war left wing authors of those post-war years and they exerted a powerful influence on my juvenile mind. It made me wonder why I was in one of the fighting services, but one didn't question parental decisions in those days and I was probably open minded enough to appreciate there was another side to the fashionable political arguments of left wing socialism.

Here are three of the war poems that affected me strongly and are typical of so many that nearly turned me into a pacifist.

Anthem for Doomed Youth
By Wilfred Owen

What passing bells for those who die as cattle?
Only the monstrous anger of the guns.
Only the stuttering rifles' rapid rattle
Can patter out their hasty orisons.
No mockeries for them, no prayers nor bells,
Nor any voice of mourning save the choirs,
The shrill demented choirs of wailing shells
And bugles calling from the shires.

The General
By Siegfried Sassoon

'Good morning, good morning!' the General said
when we met him last week on our way to the line.
Now the soldiers he smiled at are most of them dead,
And we're cursing his staff for incompetent swine.

'He's a cheery old card' grunted Harry to Jack
As they slogged up to Arras with rifle and pack.
But he did for them by his plan of attack.

The Aftermath
By Siegfried Sassoon

Do you remember the rats; and the stench
Of corpses rotting in front of the front-line trench –
And dawn coming dirty white and chill with a hopeless rain?
Do you ever stop and ask, is it ever going to happen again?

Sassoon wrote the last poem just after the end of the war in early 1919, the year I was born, and of course it did happen again twenty years later. The right timing for a baby born in March 1919.

Throughout the land there was the feeling that such slaughter must never happen again. It is difficult now (2009) to understand the universal anti-war mood in the country and the revulsion at the appalling slaughter on the Western Front. In Europe there were four million war widows and many more single women whose loved ones had been killed. Germany and France suffered terrible losses amongst their manhood. Britain suffered less because our country never became a battlefield, but we lost three quarters of a million servicemen with a further two and a half million wounded, some terribly maimed. Do we remember that Australia lost 60,000 killed and Canada 57,000, all volunteers to fight for the Empire? One and a half million Indians also fought for the British Empire. It was another world.

For my generation, growing up in the 1930s and beginning to question and think for ourselves, it was absolutely inconceivable that we should fight another war. Indeed, the concept of war to solve international disputes seemed evil. There had to be other ways of settling disputes, or so we thought.

In 1920 the bodies of four unidentifiable soldiers were dug up from the muddy landscape of Flanders and after a careful check that there was no possible means of identification one body was selected to be The Unknown Warrior to be buried in Westminster Abbey in the presence of the King and

Queen on 11 November 1920, exactly two years after the bugles sounded the 'Ceasefire' in France.

The unknown body was brought by train from France and rested overnight at Victoria Station and then taken on a gun carriage to Westminster Abbey for burial inside the Great West Door, where it lies to this day.

The tomb of The Unknown Warrior, now usually called The Unknown Soldier, was revered throughout Britain and the overwhelming emotion in the country was 'Surely Never Again'.

In 1920 a simple stone cenotaph, an empty tomb, was unveiled by the King in London in Whitehall to commemorate all the dead of the British Empire. In the immediate aftermath of the war the annual Armistice Day ceremony at the cenotaph at 11 am on 11 November, the time and date the war ended, was a hugely emotional experience. Across the land silence fell for two minutes while the dead were remembered. Trains, buses, factories and mines all fell silent in memory of the dead.

Such anti-war emotions created a mood of sincere pacifism and a yearning to make changes in society. To illustrate the strength of this feeling the undergraduates of Oxford University debating society, the Oxford Union, passed a resolution in 1933 'that this House will in no circumstances fight for King and Country'. A few years later some of them could be found amongst 'The Few' who saved their country flying Spitfires and Hurricanes in the Battle of Britain.

A League of Nations was set up, a forerunner of the United Nations, by countries hoping to preserve the peace for future generations. The League would arbitrate in disputes between nations and if necessary stop them by force. It was part of this emotional wave of a desire to avoid any more wars and I was hooked by the concept of everlasting peace. Unfortunately the Americans refused to join and the League became a toothless monster.

The first test of the League came in 1935 when Mussolini, the Italian dictator, invaded the independent kingdom of Abyssinia without any reasonable cause. Abyssinia appealed to the League of Nations and France and Britain mobilised their fleets. Our Mediterranean Fleet concentrated at Alexandria in the Eastern Med near the Suez Canal ready to close it to the Italians. We seemed about to go to war but we eventually backed down. We hadn't got the will to strike. We could easily have closed the Canal to all Italian ships and this would have stopped the war. The League's intervention fizzled out and Italy conquered Abyssinia. Hitler and Mussolini learned that it was force that counted. For me this was the beginning of a faint change of heart as I read of the merciless aerial bombardments of defenceless towns in Abyssinia.

Why, in this anti-war climate, did I join the Navy? My father was a serving naval officer. I had lived in Plymouth, the great West Country naval base, and in Portsmouth and had visited all his ships. I had watched the huge Mediterranean

Fleet steaming in and out of the Grand Harbour in Malta. Standing on the battlements of Fort St Angelo I had seen the great battleships returning to their base, bugles blaring in salute; the Royal Marine bands bashing out patriotic tunes and the smart ranks of sailors decorating the upper decks. It was a pageant of might and glory at the height of Empire.

It had been a glamorous life for a small son of a naval Commander and I was hardly surprised when my father posed the question as to my future. He and I were walking on the golf course at Gosport (God's Port) but there was nothing godlike about it.

'You will be joining the Service, I suppose,' he said. Those were his exact words.

I was eleven years of age, a mere child, more interested in stamp collecting and football and winning my first eleven colours at school. I really knew nothing about how ships worked and what duties a naval officer carried out, but the Navy was all I knew of life and I was happy to follow my father. I had never thought about an adult career or considered such a decision seriously.

'Yes,' is all I think I said and that was that.

Two years later I found myself on a special train to the Royal Naval College at Dartmouth. I soon found out.

In September 1932, no longer a civilian, I caught the Exeter train at Portsmouth (Cosham) on the London and South Western Line. In the Navy now and all dolled up in my best dark blue uniform with gilt, crowned buttons, a white shirt and stiff white collar (and what a struggle to fix it) and well shined black shoes, topped off by an officer's cap with its golden cap badge. I looked more like Little Lord Fauntleroy than a naval officer. Just thirteen years of age, I had become used to going away to boarding school for the last four years and such separations from my family were routine.

At Exeter I had to dash across to St David's station to catch the naval college special train on the Great Western Line for Kingswear. Then down the beautiful Exe estuary and across the beach at Dawlish where the sea sometimes crashes over the railway line. Strange faces were all round me – my term mates for the next four years.

We arrived at Kingswear Station, on the opposite side of the Dart from the Royal Naval College, with the rippling river just across the railway lines. We were met by a shouty Petty Officer. 'Get fell in.' Did he mean into the river to swim across with our suitcases on our heads like Sherpas? No, of course not. As we quickly learned he wanted us in two ranks so that he could try and march us to the jetty. Then up the river to the college landing steps in a naval picket boat, lugging our suitcases, green, Admiralty Pattern (very heavy) into and out of the boat.

High above us loomed the college at the top of a steep hill. Where was the bus?

'Get a hold of your suitcases and climb them steps,' shouted the Petty Officer.

'Them steps' seemed endless, hundreds of them, winding through dank trees. We made it, just.

Then straight into our dormitory to be introduced to our sea chests, a sort of open-fronted chest of drawers. My sea chest was to be my curse for the next four years. Every item of clothing had to be folded to the correct naval pattern and an exact width and length and stowed in precise piles in the chest. Shirts in one pile, vests in another, pants in another and pyjamas... and so on. Any deviations caused a major ruction with our Cadet Captains (Prefects).

Having disentangled our clothes there was a brief interlude for supper – excellent – followed by our first drill period. The next day we would be on the parade ground and we must be able to turn left and right and march off the parade. We were taken to a secluded part of the building where no one could watch our confused efforts. Just as we were finishing I passed out for a few seconds and had to sit down.

'Pull yourself together, lad,' shouted the kindly Petty Officer.

By this time I began to feel I had made a mistake in joining the Senior Service.

Early next morning we were roused and subjected to the bizarre Dartmouth routine for getting up, washing and dressing and having breakfast. We quickly learned that we did nothing until told and we stood in silence in front of our wash basins and waited for orders.

'Wash your face and hands,' called out the Cadet Captain and after what he deemed the appropriate interval for such a complex operation he shouted 'Clean your teeth'.

Surely we could manage that without an order.

Then 'Get dressed' followed by 'Say your prayers'.

There was no backsliding allowed whatever your religious preference might be. As long as you knelt and bowed your head it was assumed you were communicating with the Almighty. Prayer time was strictly regulated. Perhaps the interval was laid down in some Admiralty Manual.

Having successfully completed all these hurdles it was time for breakfast. 'At the double fall in for breakfast in the Long Corridor.'

The Long Corridor was down three flights of stairs and no meal could be started without all the college terms falling in there in two ranks in order of seniority outside the dining hall and one by one being marched into breakfast. Being the junior term we had to wait for all the other terms to march in before us. College breakfasts were sumptuous but it did involve a lot of nonsense before we could get at it. I suppose it was all part of the conditioning to make us instantly and unthinkingly obedient. This was the start of a long struggle to train a rather timid but bolshie schoolboy into a naval officer.

After breakfast there was a parade known as 'Divisions' where all the terms fell in on the parade ground in front of the college to pray and witness the ceremony of 'Colours', the hoisting of the White Ensign (the Navy's flag) at the masthead as the band played the national anthem. In pre-war days church and prayers were compulsory items of naval training, like seamanship. At 'Divisions' the order 'Roman Catholics Fall Out' was always given before we prayed, lest they be infected by the Anglican virus. They were supposed to double away out of earshot and pray on their own behind the shrubbery. Jews, nonconformists and others had to put up with the standard C of E ritual. Finally we had to march past the Captain and were subjected to the critical comments of a posse of officers.

School classes then took over from the naval ritual. To keep us fit the Navy insisted that we always doubled smartly between classes. There was always some eagle-eyed officer lurking to catch us out. 'McCrum at the double, smartly now.' Obesity was unknown at Dartmouth.

In the afternoon the college was 'cleared' and every cadet had to be out of college and taking officially regulated exercise. Anyone found indoors was punished. Exercise included any team game, cross-country running to a set course of four to five miles or an hour in the gym in the clutches of Royal Marine physical training instructors.

Like most public schools in those days team games were compulsory: there was some idea that they instilled the right attitude for running the Empire. I always thought this was a dubious principle as most of those who actually ran the Empire had a lonely existence out in the sticks as District Commissioners or Forestry Supervisors. Fishing was a much more useful pastime.

After exercise, there was tea and more classes until another parade, known as 'Evening Quarters', where each term paraded in two ranks; indoors this time on the quarterdeck, under the beady eye of a statue of King George V gazing sternly down on us. Once again we prayed rather perfunctorily, led by one of the Term Officers. On board ship 'Evening Quarters' was held at the end of the working day and the Ship's Company was 'mustered' by name to check that no one had fallen overboard. Not that anyone could have done anything about it as it might have happened any time in the previous twenty-four hours. Naval customs were sometimes mysterious. Anyway there wasn't much chance of a cadet at the Royal Naval College falling overboard and I thought it was pointless. I usually spent the time wondering what we were going to have for supper.

Meals were excellent, plentiful and well cooked and for a while we were off the leash, except that our Cadet Captains sat at the head of the table. After supper we had a spell of freedom until the ritual took over again to ensure that we got into bed in the correct naval manner. All clothing worn that day was laid out on our sea chests, neatly folded to the approved width and length. 'Say your prayers,' the Cadet Captain would shout down the dormitory where all thirty-five of us slept in strict alphabetical order, followed after a decent interval for our sacred thoughts the order 'Turn in, no more talking' and the lights went out.

Then there might follow one of the more teasing episodes of the day. If the lights stayed on in the lobby it meant a caning was about to ensue. The door would open again. 'Smith, turn out.' What monstrosity had Smith perpetrated? Swish, swish, swish – three cuts of the cane and Smith doubled very rapidly back to his bed. The crime would then be whispered from bed to bed down the dormitory and in the morning Smith would proudly display his 'marks'. So ended the day, but a caning was a comparatively rare event. I was only caned once (three cuts).

Dartmouth was a hybrid; part school, part military training establishment and the staff mirrored that set-up. The headmaster was a civilian as were all the masters but the college was under the command of a naval Captain who had overall control except for the academic areas. Young Lieutenants, fresh in from the sea, acted as Housemasters and were called Term Officers and there were a number of specialist officers and Petty Officers who trained the cadets in technical subjects.

Each term on joining the college remained segregated socially and educationally and lived together throughout their time at the college. We were not supposed to talk or socialise with any cadet in a senior or junior term, which was very restrictive if you had a friend from home above or below you. It was a highly regimented set-up. Drakes must not talk to Grenvilles and vice versa.

Within each term we were streamed into three or four classes depending on performance and moved up and down as results merited. Dartmouth offered a strange mix of normal school subjects (maths, science, history and English) and naval training in seamanship and engineering. These were interspersed with drill periods of suffocating boredom.

School terms followed the national pattern – Christmas, Easter and summer. There were no half term breaks and once the term started you were incarcerated at the college for three months. At half term parents would come down and you were given Saturday off, but not Sunday because there was a special half term parade when you marched past all the parents and the Captain, on tenterhooks lest your nearest and dearest might call out as you passed 'There's Tony, doesn't he look smart'. Or worse, your mother might be wearing inappropriate clothes or some ghastly Ascot hat. As soon as we were dismissed we hurried them off the premises and to lunch in some expensive Dartmouth hotel.

This was my life for the next four years. Looking back, it is difficult to understand why I didn't rebel. The incessant drilling and close supervision of our lives irked me and I would have enjoyed a more academic education. Yet sometimes the glamour of marching to the rousing tunes of the band and the punctilio of correctly performed drill also appealed to the emotions. We do not choose our genes as if we were shopping in Sainsbury's yet I believe they are dominant. On my mother's side there was a long line of distinguished naval Captains and Admirals as far back as the eighteenth century. In my father's family there were men and women of intellectual stature and entrepreneurial skills and no military connections except for marching at the head of the Orange Lodge marches in Northern Ireland. My father was the first member to break ranks and become a naval officer. I never had the chance to ask him why; possibly to escape the claustrophobia of Northern Ireland Protestantism.

I think I felt it was my duty to pursue a naval career. In any case, in those days (1930s), sons did not have much say in their schooling and the Navy made it difficult to get off the treadmill. If a cadet wanted 'out' his parents had to 'buy him out' and pay a large sum for the years of training he had received and for the future years when the Navy wouldn't benefit from his virtues.

I contented myself with kicking gently against the pricks and never had the guts to get up and go. There were many compensations: good friends; beautiful Devon countryside; sailing on the Dart and a total absence of bullying. So, chuntering mildly against some of the sillier aspects of naval training, I floated through the Royal Naval College, keeping my head down and avoiding my seniors. In this I was quite successful as I was never promoted to Cadet Captain (Prefect) nor did I excel sufficiently at sport to win my colours for anything. My only successes were academic, which didn't rate highly in that disciplined naval environment.

To be fair I suspect that Dartmouth did me much good. I sometimes need a sharp spur to get me going and close supervision to force me to reach my goal. I could have easily wafted around thinking beautiful thoughts and not achieving much.

Years later civilians would ask me 'Wasn't it very tough at Dartmouth?' Strangely it wasn't, not nearly as tough as my prep school nor as challenging as today's officer training. Living conditions were comfortable; the rooms centrally heated with wonderful views across the River Dart. 'Wasn't there a lot of beating'? Unlike public schools the use of the cane was carefully controlled by the Term Officer (Housemaster). No Cadet Captain was allowed to beat without his permission and the cane was sparingly used.

But there was one highly effective punishment without recourse to the cane – the *strafe*, much dreaded by cadets. This was reserved for group or mass transgressions and it didn't matter if you were personally involved or not. If there were enough sinners the whole term would be collectively punished. It was a clever torture as it could be expanded or contracted to suit the Cadet Captains.

It would start in the dormitory just before bedtime when we were weary. First the crimes were announced. 'Throwing food about in the dining hall and being rude to the catering staff.'

Then the first stage was to send the whole term down to the Long Corridor, usually a long way off in another building. There the term would be doubled up and down until breathless, followed by 'knees bend' and jumping on the spot, which was agonisingly painful.

'Up to the dormitory and change into gym clothes and back here in five minutes,' screamed the Cadet Captain.

There followed a repeat performance of exercises and then back once more to the dormitory.

'Change into No. 1s.' These were our best Sunday Parade uniforms of heavy serge and very hot.

There followed more exercises in the Long Corridor and so on until exhaustion set in. Normally there were three changes of clothes unless we had been particularly wicked. At the end of these shenanigans we were flattened, begging for mercy and boiling with hatred for our Cadet Captains.

The cleverest part of this punishment was still to come. Before getting into bed our sea chests were inspected to see that all our clothing was meticulously folded. Almost every item of our clothing had been unravelled and worn for these exercises and now lay hugger mugger all over our beds.

'Ten minutes to turn in,' shouted the Cadet Captain.

It was impossible to restow our sea chests and get undressed in that time and this was a sneaky way for the Cadet Captains to single out those they suspected as being the ringleaders.

'Smith, your shirts aren't properly folded; your chest is a mess; fall in outside.'

Then Smith and other suspected ringleaders would be subjected to more physical education, or in dire cases a caning. The strafe was a very effective punishment and we dreaded it – a pity it can't be applied to modern hooligans.

For the most heinous crimes in the college calendar, being caught *in flagrante delicto* with a female in Dartmouth, smoking or stealing there was the barbaric procedure of 'official cuts'. This was dying out in my time at Dartmouth and was only performed once and not on any of our term. It was a legacy of the cat o' nine tails – a staged ceremony. The miscreant, surrounded by the whole of his term, was marched up to the gym and there strapped by his ankles and wrists to the legs of a vaulting horse. Then the Term Officer read out the crime and sentence.

'Smoking in Mill Creek. Six cuts of the cane'.

It was nearly always six of the best but it could be more. Just before the ordeal began the term was 'turned about' so that they could hear the swish of the cane but not watch the victim. After being unstrapped the victim was marched to the sick bay to be passed 'fit for duty' or otherwise. These punishments, the strafe and official cuts, were a rarity.

The daily round of drills taught us instant obedience to orders and we seldom rebelled. We were also coached in giving orders and learned to project our voices and ourselves to a body of men, which came in handy when we became officers. Despite my dislike of our daily drills I rather enjoyed barking out orders to my term mates and seeing their immediate response to my orders. I enjoyed the sense of power, I suppose. We were gradually becoming officers who would expect such instant obedience from our men. Of course, the inculcation of discipline and instinctive reaction to orders is essential in a military service but there is a danger that constant and time-consuming parade ground drills crowd out more important learning. After all, the essence of Dartmouth training should have been to produce an able and intellectually challenging corps of officers from whom the most senior ranks of the Navy would be drawn. I felt this emphasis was lacking.

It was the sea that taught us best the necessity of instant obedience. In the summer term I sailed with my friends in Dartmouth Harbour and sometimes in the open sea. There you quickly learn the importance of alacrity to orders and giving instructions urgently and clearly. Sailing allowed you to get away from the college and 'them' and to listen to the clip clip of the waves against the bows and watch the lovely Devon coast line slip slowly by whilst chewing a delicious Mars bar. This was one of the best conditionings for our future life. The sea is a powerful and fickle mistress; one moment a gently heaving mass of blue lightly ruffled by a westerly breeze; then out of the lowering sky crashes a squall of wind, which you can see dancing towards you, throwing up horizontal lines of white spume and the boat heels over. Rapid and accurate drill is required to sail safely and hold your course. Sloppy reactions in a naval sailing whaler could lead to a capsize.

Each day we had to register a 'log' in the term logbook. A 'log' was a measure of exercise and one log had to be completed every day except Sunday. Football, rugby, hockey and cricket counted as one 'log', as did a cross-country run or an hour in the gym. Tennis or squash only counted as half a 'log' and had to be topped up by a short cross-country run or half an hour in the gym. To achieve my daily 'log' I often ran the four to five mile cross-country through the fields and over the hills above Dartmouth, as good a physical test as any game of rugby with steep hills, muddy lanes and hidden valleys. As we ran my friend Robert and I would put the Navy to rights and laugh at some of the absurdities of life in a naval college. Although we were only fifteen we were absolutely certain we knew best. Such arrogance in the young is refreshing: they soon discover their lack of judgement and understanding.

The other area in which it was deemed we needed expertise if we were to become fully fledged naval officers was ballroom dancing. In the 1930s the

Royal Navy was afloat throughout the world: in the China Seas, East Indies, South Africa, South America, the West Indies, Persian Gulf and the Mediterranean and Home waters. When 'showing the flag' in these exotic places we were expected to entertain the local bigwigs and their wives and daughters. So we had to become experts in the waltz, tango and foxtrot and, if possible, the Charleston and other way out prancings. How was this to be achieved? No women were allowed anywhere near our all-male establishment. The only officer allowed a wife in college was the Captain, and to our eyes she was well over the hill – forty-five at least.

This was the reason for one of the more bizarre segments of our training. Every Saturday evening there was a compulsory dance on the quarterdeck to the tunes of the college band. There were no women, so what did we do for partners? Two friends would pair off for the evening and shuffle round the quarterdeck, occasionally changing sex and taking the male or female part. There was no instruction so how did we learn? All I know is that by the time we left the college I was fluent in the foxtrot and waltz and nothing much else.

Thus it was that on the extremely grand occasion of the Royal Visit of His Royal Highness the Prince of Wales, later King Edward VIII of abdication fame, a very special dance was laid on. In those days a Royal Visit was an occasion of wonderment and mystique. To our amazement the heir to the throne led off on to the quarterdeck for a dance with a specially selected cadet. After two or three turns round the floor HRH took refuge in the band and seized the drumsticks and played on the drums rather expertly. Wouldn't today's tabloids have had fun with such a scenario? We didn't find this extraordinary 'carry on' of the Saturday evening dance unusual or peculiar. By now we were conditioned to accept whatever the college might throw at us. There was certainly nothing sexy about it. The only reason I danced with Bedford was that we were the same height.

Unlike many public schools at that time there was little homosexuality at Dartmouth and I was never personally aware of any episode in our term. Did we have any sex education? Absolutely none, except for one extraordinary lecture by our Term Officer, a bashful young bachelor Lieutenant and another by our parson who warned us of the perils of sex and the need to keep ourselves 'pure' until we married.

'Keep it for that wonderful day. Don't "touch" yourselves. You might go blind.'

As we had been touching ourselves for at least two years and our eyesight was still perfect we didn't believe a word of it. Looking back, it all seems incredible and I don't know why the powers that be thought that fifteen-year-olds were all really going to pay any attention to such nonsense. Anything we learned about sex came from amongst ourselves: boys with sisters or more liberated parents who passed on the word. I was left with the impression that sex was rather 'dirty' but that it was a necessary part of married life otherwise the race would die out.

Time marched on: one day much like the day before. 7 am waking and washing by numbers; breakfast; Divisions at 8.45 am; classes; dinner; games; more classes; Evening Quarters; supper; free time; prep; bed at 9 pm.

There was one disturbance to this routine, the preparation for Confirmation, which was taken seriously. Everyone got confirmed, not quite a drill but very near it. A patriarch from Exeter, Bishop William Cecil, who appeared exactly as I imagined the prophet Isaiah looked, performed the ritual. I found it deeply moving and I felt sure that God had overshadowed me and my religion became a profound influence on my life for the next twenty years. It was a most important guide during the war and until my faith was destroyed by my experiences. Perhaps it was not surprising that I won both religious knowledge prizes in my final year.

For me the most welcome and important change at the beginning of my final year was my selection for the 'Alpha' class, where cadets were allowed to specialise and to ditch unpopular subjects and had freedom from class periods, like a public school sixth form. I only just scraped in on the Headmaster's personal recommendation. He wrote 'McCrum's excellent results in History, French and English probably merit his position in the 'Alpha' class, despite his meagre results in Maths and Science.' I had recently scored nought in a Maths exam. In the eighth term exams I took the History, English and Religious knowledge prizes and also the open Naval History prize. The 'Alpha' class gave me the sort of education I enjoyed and I began to revel in Dartmouth life, but I still wasn't selected for any position of responsibility ('poor officer-like qualities, McCrum'), not even milk monitor. Many years later when I was the first in my term to be promoted to Captain RN I remembered my Term Officer's dire forecast of my abilities, but he was probably right at the time. I was a very late developer.

Towards the end of our time Drake Term was selected to represent the college at the funeral of the King-Emperor George V. Our only thought was whoopee we are going to London. There was no great emotion for the death of the Father of the Empire. We were the senior term, the only reason we had been selected, but at sixteen years of age it was exciting.

By train we travelled to the 'Smoke' and a rather grotty hotel (can't remember where) and after supper we were taken to the 'Lying in State' of the King's body in Westminster Hall. The fourteenth century Hall is one of the earliest seats of Parliament, a cavernous space with a fine hammer beamed oak roof. The queues stretched down the Embankment and up Whitehall but we were ushered in by a side entrance. In the middle of that vast space the coffin, draped in the Royal Standard, looked sadly lonely on a raised catafalque. At each corner of the coffin the four royal sons stood guard in full uniform, the new King Edward VIII, The Duke of York (later King George VI), The Duke of Gloucester and The Duke of Kent. Immobile with heads bowed over their reversed swords. In the Hall, total silence. The crowd shuffled slowly round and we joined them. It was immensely impressive as a spectacle but I cannot say I felt any emotion.

Early next morning we were roused for breakfast and warned to drink as little as possible.

'You will be standing for over four hours. No one can fall out for a pee.'

By 7.30 am we were in our allotted place in St James Street.

The death of the King-Emperor was a rallying occasion for all the countries of the British Empire. In 1936 it covered over a quarter of the planet with colonies in all the continents, looking to London as the heart of that Empire.

The Viceroy of India; the Prime Ministers of Australia, New Zealand, Canada and South Africa; Kings and Queens of Pacific Islands; Tribal Chiefs from Africa; Sultans from Arabia; Governors-General and a host of dignitaries all came together to pay homage to their dead King-Emperor.

The morning dragged on and we waited and waited. At last massed bands appeared marching down the Mall churning out lugubrious music to get us all into the appropriate solemn mood. If my memory serves me right the coffin, drawn on a naval gun carriage, appeared from the northern end of St James's Street.

The coffins of kings and queens have been drawn through the streets of London on naval gun carriages hauled by naval matelots since an earlier royal occasion when a horse drawn catafalque had broken loose and the horses had cantered off leaving the Royal Body stranded. The coffin was rescued by some sailors who then dragged it all the way to Westminster Abbey. Since then the Navy has been given the task of hauling the Royal Gun Carriage. On this day some sixty sailors held on to guide ropes and pulled the gun carriage at the slow march.

The slow march is difficult at the best of times but with the weight of the gun carriage and the coffin it requires considerable skill. It was beautifully done that day in perfect time and step to the martial music. As soon as the cortege was sighted the Drakes were called to attention and had to stand as motionless as statues until the last of the procession had passed nearly an hour later.

Would I last? I had visions of standing in a puddle in the middle of St James's Street and being taken away to be shot at dawn. What a disgrace. I concentrated on putting country names to all the royalty. Yugoslavia, Sweden. Is he Liechtenstein? And so on as they passed by.

The cortege wound its way slowly past us, the new King and the Royal Princes walking behind the coffin, followed by a galaxy of kings, presidents, prime ministers and leaders of the empire. It was like a pageant or the opening moves in a circus – a cascade of splendid uniforms. All the men marched; some obviously had never performed before. The kings of European countries followed the British Princes: Haakon of Norway (tall and gangly legged, looking like a heron), Sweden, Spain, Denmark, Italy, Greece, Romania, Bulgaria, Yugoslavia and Albania (wearing a headgear rather like the Eiffel Tower encrusted with diamonds). The Queen of the Netherlands, being a female, had to ride in a carriage and would probably have been happier on a bike.

The royal ladies, all in black, faces obscured by long black veils, jolted past in horse drawn carriages. Slow marches don't suit horses and they kept having to stop and start. The veils were worn to conceal their grief. Years later a courtier told me it also meant they could eat sandwiches without being noticed. Gazing at the carriages as they passed I wondered if Queen Mary and the princesses were consumed by grief or really rather relieved that the old boy had departed. Very irreverent but I was an irreverent sixteen-year-old. By concentrating hard on the procession I kept the pressure of the internal organs at bay.

The only light note in this lugubrious scene was the occasional horse drawing the Royal carriages relieving itself as it went along. Plop, plop, plop. The procession wound out of sight; the last of the massed bands faded into the distance.

'Well done men,' said our Term Officer. 'A good show. Right turn. Dismiss.'

It was a narrow squeak but I just made it in the mad rush to the conveniences.

We were coming to the end of what I call our shaping period. We were ready to go to sea. We had learned to obey orders and to give orders, to navigate a ship (in theory), to sail a boat, but not much about running a ship at sea or any of the arts of sailor-management. Seamanship had meant hours of boredom in a seamanship classroom twiddling with dinky little models of warships, supposed to be like real ships with the guns, winches, ropes and wires all scaled down to size. It's a personal failure of mine that when I am bored I switch off and take no further interest. I make little attempt to understand the subject and dream of happier times. I came bottom in our final seamanship exam, which obviously was an important test for a future naval officer. Four months later in the Training Cruiser I won the seamanship prize – just a difference in reality.

On the academic side the college had some fine teachers, all civilians, who gave me a love of English literature and poetry and greatly extended my knowledge of naval history. These were subjects that often helped me during the war to cling on to hope and reality. They have fed me throughout a long life and I am grateful to those schoolmasters whose own enthusiasm fired mine and still sustain me today, aged ninety.

Of the naval training classes I was naively critical at the time and still am. They were unimaginative, taught by rote and by unskilled teachers, men who had been first class Chief Petty Officers but that didn't make them inspiring teachers and officers who, likewise, had no teaching experience.

I asked my father how the officers were selected as Term Officers. He told me 'They are officers who have good reports from sea.' That didn't necessarily mean they could teach.

Overshadowing the last two years of my Dartmouth time was one of the most painful events of my life, the desertion of his family, without warning or explanation, by my father. At the time, 1934, my father was serving overseas in the Mediterranean Fleet and he wrote home to ask my mother for a divorce. He never came back to us and I only saw him three times in the next forty years. I loved him and for me this was a tragedy and it took me at least ten years to come to terms with it. The turmoil caused by his desertion and subsequent divorce affected me emotionally and this unhappiness had an effect on my final year's work. My passing out (finals) examinations disappointed me and my teachers. I took only one prize and having entered the college at No. 3 I left at No 8.

Soon the end was in sight, the end of our eleventh term, the final exams, farewell service in the chapel and a 'Leavers' Parade' where we led the college off the parade ground and marched past the Captain. Despite my hostility to some of the naval aspects of our education this was an intensely moving occasion. Emblazoned across the upper face of the college, carved in letters of stone, were the words that I had read every day that I stood on the parade ground.

'ON THE NAVY UNDER THE PROVIDENCE OF GOD THE SAFETY AND WELFARE OF THE COUNTRY DEPEND.'

We felt this strong sense of pride in our country and in our worldwide Navy that guarded it and our great Empire. We were now to become the guardians of that Empire on which the sun never set. The most lasting foundation the college had given me was a pride in my uniform and in the Navy with its wonderful history of guarding this country through time from the Armada, the wars against the Dutch and the French, the great victory off Brest on the Glorious First of June 1794 and Trafalgar.

It isn't fashionable now to express pride in our Empire but, in the 1930s, we still felt a strong pride in the Empire, which covered a quarter of the globe, with colonies in every continent. Looking back I think it was quite a feat for a small country in the North Atlantic to rule over such far flung and diverse lands.

As I caught the special train to Exeter I looked back up the hill for the last time to where the fine stone and brick buildings straddled the high ridge above the River Dart and felt elated and yet sad.

What had Dartmouth meant to me? I had somewhat unwillingly accepted naval discipline, rather as a colt being broken in eventually accepts his rider. I had grown up, but it would not have been my more mature choice of education. It was too restrictive, both socially and educationally, with its emphasis on poorly presented technical naval subjects, such as seamanship, and the mind-numbing parade ground drill. I did learn to march smartly and I could do all the known ceremonial drills – Reverse Arms, Present Arms, Port Arms and many combinations of rifle drill, which I don't remember ever doing again. I was also extremely healthy and fit. On the plus side I had discovered a love of literature and a fascination with our history. But the biggest plus was the good friendships, which lasted a lifetime.

Chapter Two

Preparation

Sea Training

A t last we were going to sea, which is why I had joined the Navy. First there was two weeks' leave and then off to Chatham to report on board HMS *Frobisher*, the cadet training cruiser, which was a cruiser specially fitted out for cadets' sea training. After four uninteresting years at Dartmouth *Frobisher* was the real thing. Away at last to sea: 'to a tall ship and a star to steer her by' (Masefield, 'Sea Fever'). Off on the far oceans, the salt of the sea on my lips, a howling gale in the rigging and scudding clouds racing overhead. Just looking at her grey hull from the dockside I was getting all excited. This was it.

It didn't take long to knock the stars out of my head. As we trooped on board our Petty Officer warned us 'Store ship today' with an evil glint in his eye. We soon found out why. In 1936 storing ship meant humping on board sacks of spuds and other foodstuffs of every description.

'Newly joined cadets fall in on the port side.'

Having nearly four years' naval experience under my belt I guessed what this segregation meant. The new boys would be allocated all the nastiest jobs. Every organisation seems to have these initiation rituals where the new boys are subjected to unpleasantnesses and the ribaldry of the older hands.

Ours was to be humping sugar. The sugar was on the jetty in huge sacks, the heaviest of the stores to be loaded. We had to stagger up the steep gangway to the deck of the ship and deposit it in the storerooms down below. And naval sugar was robust, gritty stuff, which felt like sandpaper rubbing up and down one's back. This went on for over an hour. It became sheer purgatory and all I had expected was 'a tall ship and a star to steer her by and the wheel's kick and the wind's song and the white sails shaking' (Masefield, 'Sea Fever'). Instead I had a sore back and not a line of poetry left in me.

The thrill of being on board a real ship soon made me forget the torment. At last I had a deck beneath my feet and masts pointing into the sky and all round the sea, even if it was an oily, grey mess in Chatham Dockyard. The rest of our first day was exciting as we explored the ship and found where we lived and slept until it was time to go to bed. This was another rite of initiation. At Dartmouth we had slept in beds and had never been introduced to the naval hammock, not one of your la di da garden sacks but a hard canvas job, which had to be strung up between two hooks on opposite bulkheads (walls) and it had to be stretched taut until it was flat like a bed. Inside there was a thin mattress. The hooks were about six feet above the deck and for us new boys slinging our first hammock was a nightmare. We struggled; we cursed and eventually thought we had succeeded until the Petty Officer came round.

'What's that, a sack of garbage? Rig your hammock again, properly this time.' That's how we learned, by hard experience.

Rigging the hammock is only half the problem. You still have to get into it. There it is at the level of your head; ladders are not provided. The approved method is to grab hold of the hammock lashing that ties the head of the hammock to the hook and then, with a lively leap, haul yourself up and over like a high jump athlete clearing a six foot bar. If you overdo it you land on the deck on the far side of the hammock: if you don't leap high enough you land in a heap under it.

Actually, Admiralty hammocks are extremely comfortable. No matter how much the ship rocks the hammock stays still, which keeps seasickness at bay. For the next three years my hammock was my bed. It had only one drawback, that when I got a little older and sometimes enjoyed the fleshpots ashore, it became more difficult to leap into when returning from a 'run ashore' with the joys of spring and a few pints inside me. There it is up there looking rather a long way off and very narrow. Can I make it or should I lie down underneath it on my mattress. *Nil desperandum*; I'll have a go. Up I leap, don't quite make it and fall in a crumpled heap beneath it. Try again. I hit the bullseye and land within the hammock's protective arms – all part of growing up.

Soon we were ready for sea and we sailed away down the River Medway and out into the Thames Estuary and the open sea and, at last, I got what I had looked forward to for so long. 'A windy day with the white clouds flying and the flung spray and the blown spume and the seagulls crying.' This was the start of a thirty-year love affair with the sea and now, in my old age, all I ask is a 'merry yarn from a laughing rover and quiet sleep and a sweet dream when the long trick's over' (Masefield, 'Sea Fever').

In the 1930s the class system was far more rigid than it is today (2009). No one entered Dartmouth unless he came from an independent preparatory school and I had never met a member of the working class. I had lived in a class cocoon. In our four years at Dartmouth we came across no real sailors, no denizens of the lower deck, whom one day we would command. From this secluded, artificial existence we, literally overnight, became one of the crew of *Frobisher* where we lived under lower deck conditions on a seamen's messdeck.

This was raw life where we scrubbed decks in bare feet, cleaned the brasswork, hauled on the ropes and crewed the ship – an invigorating and first class training.

We learned a lot about man-management from the examples of the officers and petty officers who commanded us. The effect of a bullying petty officer: 'Think that deck's clean; scrub it again' as he empties a bucket of dirty water all over it. Or the officer who seems not to notice you standing to attention in front of him awaiting his orders. There were also a few real able seamen appointed to stiffen us new boys who would spin unbelievable yarns of the dodges they used to fool their officers. This experience of being the underdogs in a seagoing ship was a wonderful time and made up for the artificialities of the Dartmouth training. I loved it and some of the insights I gained in the training cruiser still resonated with me thirty years later when I left the Navy.

Life on board was definitely that of a labourer and we soon picked up the language of the lower deck. Initially I was amazed at their descriptive use of the English language with the liberal use of the F and C words so that it was sometimes difficult to construe a whole sentence into something meaningful.

There was a strange dichotomy between our labouring life on board and our behaviour ashore. As soon as we stepped ashore for a spot of 'liberty' (time off) we were expected to behave as proper and polished naval officers. It was constantly impressed on us that when we went ashore we represented Our Country and the Royal Navy. A bit heavy when you are only seventeen.

Our first experience of being the Representatives of Our Country was when we arrived in Finland, the first port of call after leaving England. Remember that at Dartmouth we were never allowed out into normal society. Be seen with a girl in Dartmouth and you risked a caning, unless it was your sister. We were desperately socially unaware. Women were a strange race whom we were keen to sample, but anxious as to the correct approach. The first 'run ashore' we ever enjoyed was at Lappvik, a Finnish naval base. As this was the first time we had been let off the leash our officer felt he had to warn us about our behaviour.

'Whatever the occasion offers, enter into the spirit of things and look as if you are enjoying yourselves even if you are stoned out of your minds. Always remember, you are ambassadors: you represent the Royal Navy and your Country.' We only wanted to have a good time.

As soon as the ship arrived in port lists of entertainments offered went up on the notice boards and you put your name down for what you fancied. I decided that a picnic by a lake in the forest with a group of Finnish college students of both sexes sounded more fun than a visit to the Maritime Museum and lunch with the committee.

We met our hosts on the jetty and were bussed out to the lake. The Finns were a jolly crowd, keen to practise their English; just as well as we had not a word of Finnish. It was a hot day and the lake shimmered in the sunshine, surrounded by silver birch trees just coming into leaf.

'Would you like a bath?' enquired one of the girls. Was this an invitation? Whatever, I recalled our officer's words and was prepared to enter into the spirit of springtime. But she meant bathe.

'We have no bathing costumes,' I replied.

'Oh, in Finland you do not need costumes: we can lend you towels.'

'You mean you swim in the nude?' I enquired.

'Nude, what is that?'

'No clothes on.'

'Oh, certainly, it is lovely to feel the cold water all over your body,' she explained.

The naval visitors looked at each other and decided that, as ambassadors and representatives of the Royal Navy and Britain, we should strip off and dive straight in. We might have been swimming in the Arctic. It was not just cold but absolutely iceberg freezing and I felt as if bits were falling off me. As one we turned and rapidly swam towards the shore and saw all the Finns roaring with laughter, rolling around on the beach in hysterics, not one of them in the water. Later they told us the lake had been frozen since October and had only thawed out a few days before. After a while we saw the funny side of it and they provided an excellent picnic with plenty of beer. Soon all was forgiven and we were deposited back on the jetty in a cloud of bonhomie.

There have been hundreds of 'runs ashore' since then but I remember that one most vividly as it was my first and for being caught out. And it wouldn't be for the last time.

Of course, our life wasn't all partying. We worked hard to keep the ship clean and we stood watches on the bridge at sea as lookouts. On Saturday mornings the decks had to be 'holystoned', a peculiarly unpleasant pastime, which involved kneeling on the wooden deck in freezing water pushing a large slab of sandstone up and down the deck and then scrubbing it clean with salt water.

We took part in every activity, manning power boats, keeping watch in the engine room working the throttles, guns crews and cooking for all the cadet meals.

Our working day started at 6.30 when the rousing tones of the 'Reveille' on the bugle woke us up. 'Rise and shine, rise and shine; show a leg there; the sun's a burning your eyes out,' intoned the Boatswain's Mate over the tannoy. By the time the Reveille's final note died away we were expected to be up and lashing up our hammocks into a tight 'sausage'.

Then we scrubbed the decks until they were pristine in their cleanliness. Breakfast at last. The rest of the day was divided in two parts, physical work about the ship, cleaning, maintaining equipment and other ship's chores or classroom studies on navigation and technical subjects about the ship. The work was interesting and vivid because we could always relate it to what we saw on board. In harbour we had free time after tea at 16.00, except for a duty 'watch', which was required for various duties as they arose. It was a full day but an interesting one.

After Finland our next port of call was to be Stockholm, capital of Sweden. The approach to Stockholm took us through an archipelago of islands, pine covered and laced with lovely small sandy beaches.

'Keep your eyes skinned,' warned the regular old salts on board, 'Swedish girls bathe with nothing on.'

We knew that already from our other Scandinavian experience in Finland.

Frobisher anchored in the old harbour close to the city centre and fired a twenty-one-gun salute in honour of our hosts, Sweden. The next day the business of an official visit began. As in Finland the locals had done us proud with a host of invitations to every sort of jollification. My friend John and I chose a lunch date in the nearby university town of Uppsala with a Professor and his family. The bait was three daughters, ages fourteen to seventeen, which sounded promising. We travelled by train to Uppsala, and were met by the Professor but no girls and driven to his house. Time: one o'clock. Beautiful girls and also lovely mother. Now for food. We had been up since six scrubbing the ship clean for this important Swedish visit and we were ravenous. We chatted. Two o'clock came but no food. We chatted more. Still no food. Had we mistaken the invitation? Perhaps all they wanted to do was practise their English.

At last at 3 pm mother was in the kitchen and soon after we sat down to a fantastic meal. We should have been warned that *Middag* (lunch in Sweden) is eaten at about three o'clock, as I discovered when many years later we lived in Norway.

Lunch over, we hoped some of the girls were going to show us the delights of Stockholm. Instead, we chatted over cups of coffee. Then the Professor announced 'We are now going to the opera'.

This was obviously intended as a great treat. But not quite what two seventeen-year-old cadets were hoping for. The opera was in German. We were in a box and it was very hot and we had spent a morning of physical labour on deck. John fell asleep first as I kept pushing his head off my chest and then that terrible weight just behind my forehead warned me that I was in danger. I did try, remembering our officer's exhortations about behaviour, but I succumbed and only woke when John's snoring became so loud that I was roused.

When we were eventually deposited back on the jetty and said our farewells we felt we had failed to live up to our officer's call to be a credit to our Country and the Empire.

Wherever we cruised there were always these social occasions when we arrived in harbour and we were supposed to become experienced in handling them with aplomb and good manners. We were to be tested in every respect when we arrived in Copenhagen. 'Fifty cadets required for a luncheon invitation from HM The King of Denmark at his summer palace at Amalienborg', not far from the castle where Hamlet had lived. The King was an Honorary British Admiral. Not many volunteers to begin with: might be a bit starchy. How do you address a King? 'Your Majesty' at the start of every sentence or only at the beginning? Should we bow or curtsey or what? At least it would be different so my friend John and I decided to give it a whirl and we put our names down for the Royal Visit.

Into the coach at midday and away to Amalienborg, a beautiful Georgian-style manor house, modest in size and set amongst lovely gardens. The King met us on arrival. Far from being starchy he was delightfully informal.

'Help yourselves to food,' he said. As we had been up since 6.30 and working hard we needed no encouragement to get stuck in.

'Champagne, sir?' asked the immaculate, white-gloved waiter. This wasn't any ordinary champagne. This was Royal Vintage Champagne, a golden nectar, liquid of the gods, which slipped down with deceptive ease. We had once again been particularly warned by our officer that our behaviour must be immaculate so I thought *one* glass was permissible. It seemed to be harmless.

'I don't think another one would do any harm,' I told my friend.

'Of course not,' said John.

Time passed happily, quaffing the royal champagne, stuffing ourselves with goodies and chatting to princesses and other lovelies. I have to admit we lost count of the number of refills but they didn't seem to have much effect. I felt we were sitting on a golden cloud in a fantasy land. Magnificent King, beautiful girls and hot sunshine, perhaps a little hazy towards the end, but we were still upright and a credit to the Royal Navy, we hoped. What a fabulous party.

The coach arrived. We clambered clumsily aboard. The King waved us goodbye and off we sped back to planet earth or more precisely to sea on board the training cruiser. Another useful piece of social training.

Life wasn't always as rarefied as our royal visit and in an astonishingly short time we had learned what girls were for and Danish girls were especially beautiful. It was midsummer and it was daylight until nearly midnight and Danish youth hardly went to bed at all. They reckoned midsummer was the time for all night parties and high jinks, but not for us hardworking seagoing cadets. We had to be turned in our hammocks by 9.30 pm. It's hard to believe today: what seventeen-year-old is in bed at that time? After four years at Dartmouth we were sufficiently brainwashed to accept any rule, however daft.

It was extremely hot below decks and we were allowed to sleep on deck on our hammock mattresses. *Frobisher* was lying alongside the Langelinie Jetty where the sculpture of the Little Mermaid sits in her fountain. The jetty is merely an extension of the city streets and in the summer evenings old and young parade up and down to enjoy the cool evening air. On that evening there was more for them to enjoy: the sight of some twenty cadets in their pyjamas getting into bed. The ship rode up and down the jetty as the tide rose and fell and on this particular evening the deck was almost level with the jetty.

As we dossed down for the night the girls on the jetty called out.

'What are you doing going to bed now? Come ashore and we will give you a good time.'

They couldn't believe we really were turning in for the night.

'Are you playing a game?'

No, we were not. I heard one lovely say to her friend 'I like the look of him', but it wasn't me: one of our blond gods on the next mattress. This ribaldry went to and fro until the Duty Petty Officer put a stop to it.

'Turn in and shut up. It's after lights out.'

The sun was still high in the sky but the Navy is above such trifles.

Suddenly life had opened up for us and with the excitements of ship life at sea my thoughts about the Navy had been transformed. Steaming through the Swedish fjords with their myriad islands ringed with golden beaches was magical, or out into the wild North Sea with its horizon that went on for ever and a sky that climbed up to eternity – I was hooked. Being at sea was a new life and it remained an emotional experience for ever. Also, I felt I was being realistically trained and even the hard physical work was enjoyable.

Our autumn cruise was going to be to the West Indies but suddenly it was cancelled. I was devastated because the West Indies cruise was considered to be the best. The reason was that the Government had woken up to the fact that Germany was rapidly re-arming. It had marched into the Rhineland early in 1936 in defiance of the Versailles Peace Treaty, which had stipulated that it was to remain de-militarised. The Navy was to be increased in size and the entry of young naval officers had to be doubled and the quickest way was to increase the numbers selected from the public and grammar schools at age eighteen. It would take nearly four years to increase the number of Dartmouth cadets coming to sea. It intrigued me to find that these eighteen-year-olds could become fully fledged midshipmen after only eight months in the training cruiser and were then just as good as the Dartmouth cadets after four years of naval training. It reinforced my opinion that much of the Dartmouth training was unnecessary and out of date. I wished I could have gone to a public school. I was moaning about my lack of education to an ex-public school cadet, always known as 'Pubs', when he surprised me when he said 'You must remember we look upon you Darts as the yardstick against which we measure ourselves'.

In September 1932 I had arrived at Dartmouth as a thirteen-year-old child and by the end of 1936 I was a half trained and eager young man. After the doubts and travails of my Dartmouth years I had discovered a love of the sea and this reconciled me to the occasional absurdities and stupidities of a closely disciplined and regimented existence. I had become a naively opinionated and arrogant young man who would learn by experience how wrong some of his opinions were.

So instead of a second term in the training cruiser the whole of my Dartmouth Drake Term was shunted off to a 29,000-ton battleship in Plymouth, HMS *Royal Oak*. She had eight 15-inch guns and a twelve 6-inch secondary armament and large numbers of anti-aircraft weapons. She had recently been modernised and was now considered to be ready for anything that modern warfare could throw at her. She was sunk in the first weeks of the war in Scapa Flow in the Orkneys with the loss of 853 lives.

I was to serve in her from September 1936 to January 1939 throughout my midshipman's time until the date of my promotion to Acting Sub Lieutenant (my first gold stripe). But now I was only a young (seventeen) Seagoing Cadet reporting for duty to the Officer of the Watch on a vast quarterdeck and feeling lonely and very small.

'Cadet McCrum reporting for duty, sir.'

'Stow your gear in the midshipmen's chest flat and report to the Sub Lieutenant.'

'Aye aye, sir', I replied.

We never said 'yes'. It had to be the twice repeated 'Aye Aye', the repetition of the words made sure you really did mean 'Yes' and had understood the order. Everything looked huge; massive gun turrets towered above the quarterdeck and the bridge structure reared up into the sky like a castellated castle. I was thrilled, if a little over-awed.

I came to learn over the years that ships weren't impersonal steel structures, but alive with personalities of their own. All sailors know this. There is some extraordinary aura that each ship develops, almost human, that has an effect on all who sail in her. Years later when I was appointed to HMS *Concord* a friend told me 'She's a very happy ship'. What more could a skipper want? And she was happy and made me and all my crew happy too. Other ships develop different personalities. 'She's a Jonah', an unlucky ship, much to be dreaded, or 'Proper Bounty', a very unhappy ship teetering on the edge of mutiny. Hence Captain Bligh and *Bounty*.

Quickly your ship embraces you and she becomes your home. The Captain sets the tone and morale of a ship. *Royal Oak* wasn't a particularly happy ship but she was extremely efficient and that is most important. Then the groups within a ship also have a powerful effect on one's daily life. The 'gunroom' is a peculiar group, which comprises the young officers of the future, known as midshipmen (mids), who work and live in the gunroom which, in the days of sail, was a space below the upper gun deck. In modern times it is merely a room where the mids eat, drink, work and spend their leisure time.

All this was in front of me. I could not foresee the excitements, failures and triumphs that lay ahead in the coming two and a half years. Now I had to find the chest flat and unpack and then meet the rest of the term in the gunroom. Life was different from *Frobisher*. We no longer scrubbed the decks and laboured as lower deck seamen. We were definitely young officers in the making and gunroom life was totally different to our life in a broadside mess in the training cruiser.

Our training was a mixture of classroom and practical. We took charge of motor boats and stood our watch on the quarterdeck in harbour and on the bridge at sea and occasionally we were allowed to steer this great behemoth, which gave me a feeling of great power as I turned the wheel and I could watch the ship's bows moving at my command. In my time on board I visited every compartment from the crow's nest up the mast to the bilges under the lowest deck. Of all my ships I think I knew *Royal Oak* most intimately.

Every week we had to write a description of what had occurred in the ship or fleet and to produce a fine linear sketch of one of the ship's operational systems such as the fire mains. We were not expected to express our personal opinions and I sometime got into trouble as I could not resist making my views known. At that time I had strong left wing views, which were not quite the thing in naval circles. Our Captain read the journals every week and this is the sort of comment I received from him.

'Accuracy and facts are better than imagination in a journal of this sort. You take trouble but seem inclined to want to be a sensationalist. Not a good line.' A sensationalist was someone who expressed political views.

If we had only known it World War II was starting. On 21 July 1936 the Spanish General Franco, in command of the troops in Morocco and the Spanish Islands, landed an invading army in southern Spain to overthrow the legitimate Spanish Government. It was a left wing government with communist leanings and was supported by Russia. Although the Government had been democratically elected it was opposed by the Church, which was very powerful, and also by the aristocracy. Furthermore, the German and Italian dictators, Hitler and Mussolini, supported Franco. This was the start of the vicious civil war, which lasted for three years. It also divided Europe into warring camps, Communism versus Fascism.

Britain and France were mandated by the League of Nations to preserve a neutrality, which was impossible to enforce because force was ruled out. The Navy spent many fruitless months patrolling the coasts of Spain to prevent arms being landed for the use of either side. The French and ourselves were supposed to be a sort of referee to see fair play. Some hope, but what it did do was to introduce us to the critical effects of air power as we watched the aerial bombardments of Palma and Valencia. We were left in no doubt of the potency of air power. It was our introduction to modern warfare.

Sometimes when we were on patrol we were mistaken by the war protagonists as 'enemy' ships and we were once bombed by Spanish Government planes but they missed by at least 200 yards. At sea we got used to cruising at war stations with some guns manned and by night the ship was blacked out. Slowly we were being prepared for war, but to my generation war still seemed impossible. Surely never again. All around us we could see the evils of war. One night a Franco cruiser bombarded the defenceless city of Valencia for hours, firing directly over our heads, but well to seaward of us. On another occasion we were ordered into Valencia to collect some refugees fleeing from the massacres by Government forces. Only three out of the 100+ we were expecting arrived. The rest had been slaughtered on the way. One of our jobs was to collect refugees, especially women and children, of either side and take them to places of safety. We spent many boring hours at 'Action Stations' when we were near warships of either side. At 'Action Stations' I had to descend three decks down to the bowels of the ship to what was known as the 6-inch clockroom. The so-called clock was a large computer in a small compartment where I was in charge of a team of sailors. Our job was to operate the computer, feeding it with the enemy's course and speed and range, which were passed down to us from rangefinders and spotters on high. Applying these to the computer we could then tell the 6-inch batteries what elevation and aim off to apply to the guns. This was my first taste of a small command and I greatly enjoyed it. The guns were only fired in practice shoots but it was a big thrill when all six guns went off at once. During our many months on the Spanish patrols we often had to go to 'Action Stations' in earnest when one of the Spanish warships threatened one of our merchant ships, but we never had to fire our guns in anger as the 'enemy' ships always gave way and moved off.

Here is a typical example of an evening off the North Spanish coast near Santander taken from my journal. Santander was in Government hands but the Franco navy was blockading it off shore.

Usual routine. Action Stations. The British ship 'Marvia' left Santander with refugees and her passage had been arranged and she was unmolested. Shortly after 1900 planes could be seen leaving the shore. We knew them to be Government planes as Cabo Mayor wireless station had sent the following message to 'All British Men of War'.

'Rebel ships shall be bombed. Have silhouette of your ships. Will not drop bombs on English ships.'

This was quite a relief but any attacking aircraft would have got a hot reception as all our anti-aircraft guns were at the ready.

The Spanish Civil War was a cruel war. Both sides killed each other indiscriminately and the appalling aerial bombardment of Guernica by German aircraft was typical of the barbarity. The more we saw of the horrors that war unleashed the more we hoped we could avert another world war. Despite the tardy and half hearted rearmament programme that our government launched in 1935 the country and particularly the young was still strongly pacifist. For myself I was still weighed down by the baggage of World War I and its obscenities. I did not want to contemplate fighting and the civil war in Spain reinforced those feelings.

As an important part of our 'seasoning' to become proper officers we had to spend three months in a destroyer to understand life in a small ship and my friend John and I were appointed to HMS *Basilisk* in the autumn of 1937. *Basilisk* was a fast destroyer of 1,300 tons and a complete contrast to the massive *Royal Oak*. She gave us excellent training as we understudied every officer on board in succession and we lived in the wardroom with the ship's officers, the first time we had been able to socialise with men with gold stripes on their arms. I learned far more listening and talking to these destroyer officers than from formal instruction.

Our Captain was a fiery redhead, Teddy Dangerfield, who became over excited at what seemed to me trivial matters. But it was only a storm in a teacup, which blew away sharply.

One morning off the south-east coast of Spain, where we could see the little fishing villages nestling under the backdrop of inland hills now the Mecca of cheap holidays for many Brits, we were on patrol. The operator on the anti-submarine equipment shouted 'Hydrophone effect to starboard' and shortly afterwards a torpedo track was sighted coming towards us. Hydrophone effect is underwater noise from a submarine or torpedo or also from some fish or a shoal of fish. Our skipper leapt into action and we loosed off numbers of depth charges to destroy the 'enemy'. All very exciting and the *Daily Mirror* blazoned headlines a few days later: 'BRITISH DESTROYER ATTACKED BY UNKNOWN SUBMARINE.'

We spent all morning searching for the mystery attacker and depth charging and destroying the fish life of the Mediterranean and then we were ordered to return to Gibraltar. We had escaped unharmed. A more mature consideration of the event suggested that the torpedo track was that of a school of porpoises. In World War II we frequently detected schools of fish, which closely resembled submarine or torpedo noise, and our anti-submarine operators learned to distinguish them, but it was fun while it lasted. While our time off the Spanish coasts in 1936, 1937 and 1938 taught us what war was like there were happier interludes when we went into Gibraltar and enjoyed the shore life, playing hockey, squash and tennis and entertaining friends from other ships and carousing in the cafes in the canyon-like main street. Another world from the horrors of the civil war. Surely this was how life should be, not maiming and killing and destroying. Surely world war must be avoided.

One day my friend John and I decided to climb to the top of the Rock of Gibraltar. On the way up we passed the famous Rock monkeys who were carefully nurtured because it was believed that if they died out the British Empire would come to an end. Well, they are still there (2009) but the Empire has long passed away.

John and I much enjoyed our destroyer months and learned a lot. I found the more intimate life on board most congenial and decided that I would aim to become a destroyer officer in the future. We went back to our battleship more rounded young men.

In the spring of 1937 and 1938 the two largest fleets of the Royal Navy, the Mediterranean and the Home Fleet, met at Gibraltar for the great annual exercise 'battles' between the fleets when the latest tactical ideas were tried out. The Red Fleet (Home) fought it out with the Blue Fleet (Med) to train the crews and officers and Captains in modern warfare. Unfortunately, most of these encounters were merely re-runs of the battles of World War I, Jutland and Dogger Bank. With hindsight it is difficult to see how the Navy's top brass failed to appreciate the might of air power. This failure was to result in many of the heavy casualties in the early years of World War II, off Norway, at Dunkirk, Dieppe and Crete. The worst naval blunder of the inter-war years was our concentration on the battleship and the neglect of the Fleet Air Arm and the aircraft carrier. Many lives were lost unnecessarily.

I believe the younger officers were more aware of the air threat than their seniors because we weren't lumbered with a World War I experience. At the end of these 'battles' the officers of both fleets assembled in what were the old coal sheds, where in the days of coal propulsion, ship's coal was stored. There the Admirals and their staffs would describe their actions and their reasons for their decisions. It was most interesting for us youngsters and an amazingly open and educative discussion, much to the credit of the top brass. Questions could be asked but few of us midshipmen dared to doubt the omniscience of all those gold stripes. However, I remember one bold young Fleet Air Arm pilot who drew attention to the fact that a large number of aircraft had targeted the battleship squadrons and would have disabled or sunk many ships.

'Nonsense,' rebutted the Admirals almost as one, 'the anti-aircraft guns would have shot them all down.'

Many of us felt mighty dubious and eventually we were proved right as the sinking by Japanese aircraft of the battleships *Prince of Wales* and *Repulse* in 1942 showed. In war, anti-aircraft guns proved remarkably ineffective and the only successful defence of ships at sea was from fighter aircraft, either based in carriers or ashore.

In March 1938 Hitler marched his armies into Austria with the encouragement of the majority of the Austrian people.

These were the years that became known as the Appeasement when Britain gave way to the demands of the dictators and they concluded we were decadent and would never fight. I remember listening to Hitler's speeches to mass gatherings of Nazis. Row upon row of them in brown uniforms with the crooked cross of the swastika on their armbands. He had a harsh, hypnotic voice and on the radio it sounded as if he was screaming at his audience. He used his pauses and the crescendo of his sentences with great skill and repeatedly brought his audience to the boil and they sounded like the baying of wild animals with their shouts of '*Sig Heil, Sig Heil*' constantly repeated. It was electrifying and terrifying.

Stories were coming out of Germany about the baiting of the Jews. We knew they had to wear a large yellow J on their clothes and we heard terrible stories of the mistreatment of mentally defective children. Yet there were some amongst the right wing of the Conservative Party and the minor aristocracy, like Sir Oswald and Lady Mosley, who believed in Hitler. All they saw was that he had restored order and reduced unemployment and given the Germans faith in themselves. They were blind to the cruelties and obscenities of the Nazi thugs. Both Sir Oswald and Lady Mosley were imprisoned during the war.

Only Churchill was trying to warn the public of the dangers of Nazism but he was written off as a warmonger. The young did not doubt that the Nazis were evil but we still hoped to avoid having to fight. We were foolishly naïve.

By the middle of 1938 rearmament in Britain was in full swing: the Royal Navy and the Royal Air Force were being rapidly increased but it takes three years to build a ship and, at sea, we didn't see much progress.

In September 1938 Hitler declared that his patience with Czechoslovakia was exhausted. He wanted an excuse to invade her and retake the Sudetenland, which had been taken from Germany after World War I. War seemed imminent and the British Reserve Fleet was mobilised and ships were moved to their war stations. We were on the brink of World War II. Neville Chamberlain, the Prime Minister, flew to Germany to deter Hitler and with the French Prime Minister a deal was cut. We surrendered the Czech people to the predator and the Sudetenland was occupied by the German army. Chamberlain flew back to Britain, waving a piece of paper and calling out 'Peace in our time'. It lasted eleven months. He had been diddled by Hitler, but except for Churchill and some of his friends the country happily supported Chamberlain as did most of my generation. I was relieved that we didn't have to fight and, somehow, we deluded ourselves that maybe we wouldn't have to. We were still so affected by the appalling casualties of the Great War that we clung to the hope that peace would prevail.

It is easy to see now that Appeasement was a false policy, but the majority of the British and French people were not ready for war. Lack of guts? I don't think so. We were so oppressed by the ghosts of those doomed soldiers on the Somme, at Passchendaele, at Gallipoli and in Russia that we wanted to be absolutely certain another war was really necessary.

I believe that final year, September 1938 to September 1939, eventually hardened our will and we came to accept that there was no way out except to fight. By the time we declared war on Germany on 3 September 1939 I was absolutely convinced that we had to fight. All doubts had been swept aside. Like my generation I was by then totally prepared for war. That final year was probably necessary to fire us young for the sacrifices ahead. After all it is the young who bear the load of casualties in war.

In December 1938 we sat our final exams in *Royal Oak* and a few days before Christmas we left the ship, which had been our home for more than two years. It was sad to say goodbye to that grey battleship, so solid and reassuring. I can still recall that distinctive ship smell of linoleum floor polish and Brasso that pervaded the area where I slung my hammock. Returning from shore after an evening's leave the wide quarterdeck, silent except for the slap of the Officer of the Watches feet as he walked slowly up and down, gave me a feeling of total security and of invulnerability. Yet a year later *Royal Oak* lay on the bottom of Scapa Flow in the Orkney Islands, a coffin for 853 of her crew.

Our Dartmouth training had been a time of conditioning, of breaking in to a stern discipline and acceptance of a rigid existence. The past three years as cadets and midshipmen had given us a varied experience of the sea and seamanship in all its forms and an understanding of human relationships.

We had seen the might of the oceans when *Royal Oak* had battled her way through hurricane force winds in the Bay of Biscay. Almost disappearing into the swell one minute and then shaking the sea off her inundated decks as she crested the waves and away to starboard two aircraft carriers, looking more like submarines than huge surface ships as they disappeared from sight into a mighty wave. A wonderful lesson in nature's strength.

It was a thrill to steer a 29,000-ton battleship in rough weather and we learned much from the many hours we stood watch on the bridge on passage and during exercises, observing how the Captain and the Officers of the Watch performed under pressure. On the long night watches a good Officer of the Watch would talk to you and explain his thoughts and actions, a fine piece of informal training Some of the younger officers were excellent and natural teachers. Likewise, as Midshipman of the Watch in harbour, pacing the quarterdeck with the Officer of the Watch and coping with minor crises that arose, small fires, drunken libertymen and minor defaulters, we absorbed many of the arts of good man management.

Probably the finest training in seamanship and man management was when you were allocated to be the skipper of a boat. My first boat was an open launch, some forty feet long and used to ferry libertymen from ship to shore and back again. There was no cover and the boat was open to the wind and sea, a bracing experience. My first command and I was only seventeen but up for it. The challenge was the return journey at 11 pm after the libertymen had had a solid evening's drinking in the pubs of Weymouth. The Petty Officer and I were required to return some sixty jolly tars back to the ship in Portland Harbour in a shipshape and orderly manner and especially no singing. My technique was the softly softly approach. Let them rip away with their shanties as we left

Weymouth Harbour and out into the open sea but as soon as we entered Portland Harbour, where the fleet was at anchor, discipline had to be restored. It would be a black mark for young McCrum if he delivered a posse of drunken matelots alongside the gangway singing ribald verses of 'The Good Ship Venus'.

'Silence in the boat; silence in the boat,' I shouted over the uproar. No one takes a blind bit of notice of this juvenile officer. So I turn the launch into wind and sea.

'Shut up,' I shout again in my posh Dartmouth voice, which is certain to be mimicked up for'd. 'I shall steer into the wind until you are completely silent,' and with that accelerate into the wind and sea until the spray is coming over the bows and gently cooling the front rows.

Very quickly there is total silence and I ease off and head for the ship. 'Absolute silence when we get alongside,' I remind them again but they are all now suitably cowed and climb up the gangway like a gaggle of penguins. I soon had this routine taped and enjoyed my trips to and from Weymouth in the dark night.

The next step up the ladder was when you were selected to command a picket boat. These boats had all the ingredients of a larger ship; a boiler room where steam was raised to power the engine and passenger spaces amidships and right aft to seat the passengers, including a cabin for use in rough weather. Apart from me there was a crew of four, a seasoned Petty Officer as Second in Command and to watch over the young, inexperienced midshipman skipper; an engineer; a bowman and a sternsheetman with boat hooks to grapple with the gangway.

Picket boats took officers ashore and to other ships. So the mid was always under close scrutiny, particularly when the officers were returning to the ship after an evening ashore and felt moved to offer helpful ship handling hints, of which I took absolutely no notice.

Running boats was exciting as you got away from the ship and learned practical ship handling skills. In rough weather it was an art to bring the boat alongside the ship's gangway with the swell rising and falling five or six feet. If you made a hash of it the Officer of the Watch on the quarterdeck would call out 'Round again McCrum' and you would have to cast off and make a full circle and come up alongside the gangway again. If your nerve broke you might have to do it three or four times.

Perhaps the greatest value of boat running was the opportunity to talk and listen to the crew as we sometimes spent long hours waiting alongside the jetty ashore. Another useful perspective on lower deck life. I spent many months running boats and the experience taught me how to handle ships' boats in all weathers and was a great confidence builder.

During these two years we became intimately involved in every seamanlike activity on board. How to drop and raise the huge anchors; how to fix the ship's position by the stars; how to signal by semaphore and flashing lamp; how to lower and raise the ship's boats and how to fight the ship. Throughout this time we were growing in knowledge and confidence and gaining an understanding of the ways of the lower deck. Slowly, imperceptibly we learned our trade, the technical skills, the people skills and our own weaknesses in character and skill. It was an amazing experience to spend two years when we could make mistakes without causing too much harm and where the sailors were more open to you than when you became a proper officer with stripes on your arms.

After our two years of mid's time there wasn't much I didn't know about the technicalities of running a warship, at least in theory. At last I felt I had salt in my blood and I was at home on the sea and had learned to respect it. The time of Preparation was over and, trained by the sea, we were ready for our commissions and first gold stripes.

I had come a long way since September 1932 when a timid thirteen-year-old had arrived at Dartmouth. Seven years later our basic training was complete. I had a First Class Certificate under my belt and I felt self-assured and ready for life as a Commissioned Officer with one gold stripe on each arm. On 1 January 1939 I 'shipped' my first stripe as an Acting Sub Lieutenant RN.

A few months ashore in Portsmouth completing advanced technical training in navigation, weapons, electrics and signals and we were ready to man any ship in the Navy, battleship, cruiser or destroyer. I knew I was now fully trained. It had taken a long time but thereafter there was never a time in twenty-five years of naval service when I did not feel in control of my job.

Halfway through these technical courses the war noises from Germany became more insistent. The drums of war were beating loudly. The Drake Term was at the Gunnery School where we were learning all about modern weapons and also spent much time strutting around on the parade ground repeating drills we had endlessly undergone at Dartmouth. It really was a waste of our precious time when there was so much to be learned about weapons and tactics. We were, after all, supposed to be training as officers not automata.

Back to the Gunnery School parade ground, our course officer appeared.

'From here to the left, left turn, quick march and fall in in the drill shed. From here to the right stand easy.'

And that decided our fate for the first two years of the war. Those in the drill shed went to sloops and minesweepers and those on the parade ground went to destroyers. I was in the left hand group and was told to report to HMS *Skipjack*, mouldering in reserve in Chatham Dockyard. The threat of war meant that all mothballed ships (the Reserve Fleet) were being brought to readiness for war.

The next day I drove my recently acquired Morris Tourer (£17) to Chatham and found *Skipjack* in dock, rusty and dirty after years in reserve. I was told to leave my car in the local barracks garage and didn't see it again until 1946, when, with new batteries, it went perfectly.

Chapter Three

Apprehension

Preparing for War

HMS *Skipjack* was a fast fleet minesweeper, designed for safe minesweeping and to sweep ahead of a fleet. She had two 4-inch guns and some anti-aircraft machine-guns, depth charges for attacking submarines and anti-sub detection gear. I had never been in such a small ship, even smaller than a destroyer, just over 1,000 tons' displacement, about the size of the modern Isle of Wight ferry. She was filthy. Our first task was a simple housekeeping job, getting the ship clean inside and out. She had been mothballed some years before and needed a coat of paint and much scrubbing.

The Ship's Company consisted mostly of men who had left the Navy some years before and had been called up for the emergency: postmen, grocers, butchers, builders, painters and decorators. A liquorice all sorts crew who had been on the reserve after serving in the Navy for either twelve or seven years. There was also a smattering of young National Servicemen and Royal Naval Volunteer Reservists, mostly from the City, bank clerks, insurance salesmen and traders from the stock exchange, all eager to learn and prove themselves as good as the regulars. I had the privilege of training some of them to become officers and mostly they did well, because of or in spite of my efforts. There were few regular naval ratings. It was a motley crew enlivened by a large number of cockneys amongst the naval reservists as Chatham-based ships were mostly crewed from London and the Home Counties. They proved to be a hilarious bunch as they had less reverence for the minutiae of naval discipline than regular sailors and they had a wicked wit, which they sometimes took out on their officers behind their backs. The Captain had also been recalled to the colours after several years 'on the beach'. The First Lieutenant (2nd in Command), always called 'No. 1' by the officers and 'Jimmy the One' or just plain 'Jimmy' by the sailors, but not to his face of course, had been promoted from the lower deck. He had been an Able Seaman for several years and knew all the tricks and dodges of the matelot. He was a well trained seaman, knowledgeable in the arts of seamanship and easy to get on with, but we were not soul mates. The Engineer, known as 'Chiefie' (for Chief Engineer), looked to me as old as Methuselah but was in his late forties and, sadly, was killed at Dunkirk. He also had been recalled after many years ashore. Lastly there was me, young, Dartmouth trained, and probably rather smug. Despite getting on well with my fellow officers I had little in common with them and was closer in age and interests with some of the young Royal Naval Volunteer Reserve ratings I was training to become officers, but naval convention and the fact that they lived on the lower deck prevented me socialising with them. I was to be the navigator, signal officer, Captain's Secretary and general office dogsbody. We were very short of officers and for the next four months I seldom had a spare moment. Surprisingly, considering the majority of the crew had been torn away from their civilian world, they worked cheerfully to get the ship clean and all the machinery and equipment working effectively. Within a week the ship was ready for sea, but first we had to get out of Chatham Dockyard and down the River Medway to Sheerness. As the ship got under way my station as navigator was by the voicepipe on the bridge to relay the Captain's orders to the helmsman in the wheelhouse below and to the engine room. As we left the dock to enter the narrow river channel we had to make a particularly sharp turn to starboard (to the right) to shape course down the river. To my amazement the Captain ordered 'Hard a Port' (to the left), which would put the ship firmly on to the mud on the steep left bank of the river. There was no time for explanation or argument. I shouted down the voicepipe. 'Cancel the last order. Hard a Starboard.' Naturally the Captain was furious that his young navigator had countermanded his orders. As the ship's bows swung back to starboard I ordered 'Amidships' to bring the wheel back to the centre and the ship heading down the river. By this time the Captain realised his mistake and we both understood what had gone wrong. Some years before when the Captain was at sea the helm orders were as they had been in sailing ship days. Wheel to port meant the ship's bows went to starboard and vice versa. Instinctively, the Captain had used the old orders, which I had heard about but never used. It was bad luck on the skipper that he had made such a potentially dangerous mistake on his first outing but he bore me no malice. However, it made me appreciate how out of touch he was with the modern Navy and the story went round the ship in no time. I'm afraid he lost the confidence of many. He was a remarkably pleasant man socially who had been a political agent since leaving the Navy, but he was nervous and this showed him up on the bridge. One thing a Captain must not be is nervous. He must always appear calm and in total control of any mayhem that may be going on around him. He was a visibly 'nervy' man who, when worried, would rub his palms together in agitation and much as I liked him I had no respect for him. He didn't fill the role that my training told me a Captain should. Unfortunately the Ship's

Company had the same lack of respect. He was an honest man, trying to do his best. It must have been a terrible strain on him.

When we were in harbour I ran the ship's office, the administrative hub, where I struggled to keep the accounts and where correspondence to and from august naval bodies was prepared. The office equipment was antediluvian; an ancient typewriter and a duplicating 'jelly' if more than three copies of a document were required. To duplicate documents you first had to heat a strange liquid and pour it into a shallow tray and wait for it to cool and solidify, then the letter or whatever was pressed down on to the jelly, which then had the text imprinted on it and lo any number of copies could be run off. A miracle of modern science. I also had to pay the Ship's Company in cash and calculate each man's pay and envelope it and hand it out on pay day. The sums never seemed to add up and I often had to fork out a quid or two to make the accounts balance. Maths had never been my strong subject. None of these admin tasks had been covered at Dartmouth but out of chaos and much practice order emerged but I was glad when we went to sea and I could become the navigator for which I had been well trained.

It was exciting as we slipped out of Sheerness and into the busy Thames Estuary, teeming with shipping and laced by many narrow channels, rather like the veins of a body, leading out to the open sea. The Thames, the Medway, the Crouch, the Blackwater and the Colne rivers all channelled into the estuary and as they met the North Sea produced sandbanks along the coast, a trap for the unwary navigator.

We were soon out into the North Sea and my first tricky bit of navigating as we threaded our way through those sandbanks off the Essex coast. Our destination was Harwich where we were to join up with the rest of the 2nd Minesweeping Flotilla and from then on we usually formed part of this family of minesweepers, which consisted of six ships working together to sweep mines. Harwich was a fishing port and the cross channel ferry harbour for the Dutch and Belgian ports, a drab place on the River Stour with lots of pubs and not much else and across the river a famous naval training school for fifteen and sixteen-year-old boys destined for the lower deck of the Royal Navy, HMS *Ganges*.

Little did I know that eighteen years later I would be the Second in Command of HMS *Ganges* and just married and living right on the river banks with a screaming three-month-old baby.

In June 1939 there was no doubt that war was imminent and we had to be ready. The 'work up' was hard and unrelenting. Each day we steamed out of harbour at dawn and our navigation had to be extremely accurate as we had to exit down a long tortuous channel closely following in the wake of one of our sister ships. As soon as we were clear of the coast the flotilla streamed their sweeps: then we formed up the six ships of the flotilla and worked up and down a dummy minefield with sand-filled mines. Streaming sweeps is the unwinding of the minesweeping wires, which are towed astern of the ship to cut the mooring wires of the undersea mines.

This was my first taste of navigating and it was exciting and fun to be, at last, applying one's knowledge and skills. I still had one more hurdle to leap before I became a fully qualified commissioned officer. Sub Lieutenants were only Acting Sub Lieutenants until they had completed a minimum time as a watchkeeper on the bridge of a ship at sea and passed by the Captain 'as fit to take charge of a watch without supervision'. This was a certainty unless you were rude to your Captain or were found drunk on watch. I managed to avoid these snares and after a few weeks received my watchkeeping ticket.

Our mixed bag of officers and men now had a short time to become proficient minesweepers as war was looming. We were all learners and the ship should have worn L plates. None of us had any experience of sweeping mines and I suspect we were all apprehensive about what the future might bring. In World War I the casualties in minesweepers had been the highest in the Navy and many sweepers had been sunk by the mines they were trying to clear. Since then specialised sweepers, such as *Skipjack*, had been designed and in World War II minesweeping was much safer.

We learned how to sweep the dummy mines, filled with sand, but just like the real thing. We practised firing our guns, fighting fires, repairing damage and we got ready for war. It was no longer a question of whether war would break out but when. Every day my personal routine was much the same: on the bridge at first light, navigating the ship out of harbour and into the wide seas beyond. The North Sea is not a favourite of mine, grey and cold even in summer.

The Suffolk and Norfolk coasts are flat and featureless with long sandbanks running parallel with the coast, protecting it like ramparts round a castle. It was easy to run aground.

Apart from a quick break for lunch I spent the day on the bridge, plotting the ship's course and fixing her position by taking compass bearings of lightships and shore marks. Churches were a great help with their high steeples. It needed concentration but it was satisfying and I enjoyed it. It was what my previous seven years had prepared me for and I felt absolutely confident. When you are only twenty and well trained you really think you know it all. It never occurred to me that I was still pretty inexperienced.

Being constantly at sea brought the Ship's Company into a close knit fraternity and we soon knew each other well, our strengths, weaknesses and failings. None of us had any battle experience. Although many of the seamen and stokers had served in the Navy for twelve years none had war experience. We were very short of officers and when we were minesweeping the First Lieutenant was fully engaged on the sweep deck so I was the only bridge watchkeeper. Throughout June, July and August we were hard pressed and when we got back to harbour in the evening there was always correspondence to tackle and charts to correct. My feet hardly touched the shore that summer.

Despite the hard work we had the satisfaction of seeing the ship and the other ships in our flotilla becoming efficient minesweepers, ready to tackle any wartime task. We never spoke openly about our fears for the future. I think that in those last few weeks before war broke out we were all screwing down on our emotions so that we could face the uncertainties of war with some aplomb.

By the end of July we were considered fully worked up and ready for active service. We left Harwich with no regrets: it was a dreary place where it had been nothing but work, work, work. We were on our way to Dover, our war station. We were ready.

Once we got to Dover minesweeping started in earnest. Our minelayers were laying deep mines to seal off the narrow Dover Straits to prevent German submarines trying to sail out into the Atlantic when war started. This would force them to go round the north of Scotland and use up time and fuel. The mines had to be laid very carefully at a depth that would allow surface ships to pass safely over the top of them and only catch the submerged submarines below. The Dover straits had the largest concentration of shipping in the world. What a furore there would be if a neutral ship blew up on a British mine. Our job was to skim over the top of each line of mines to make sure the depth setting of every mine was correct and if one was too shallow to sweep it up. Then the mine would come bobbing to the surface and we would try to blow it up by shooting at the detonators. It required great accuracy of sweeping to cut the mine mooring wires of the shallow mines and leave the deep ones undisturbed.

Our flotilla left Dover in the early summer mornings when the first pink glow of dawn rose out of the sea and it would be light enough to see the float that marked the end of our minesweeping wires. The minefield began near the South Goodwin Lightship off Ramsgate and then we swept up and down the lines of mines all the way to Cap Gris Nez near Calais. As soon as we got out to the minefield area we streamed our sweeps and continued sweeping until evening.

On a typical day with Dover's white cliffs astern of us and the grey cliffs of Gris Nez ahead all we had to do was to keep in formation and watch the dolphin–like float of the ship ahead which marked the end of her sweep wire and our own float astern of us, which marked the end of our sweep wire. If our float dipped under the sea there was either a mine in the wire or a piece of wreckage or other bit of rubbish. Then all eyes strained to look for a possible mine surfacing. Up it comes like some football bouncing along the waves looking rather jolly. It's my first live mine, even if it is a British one. British mines make just as big a bang as German ones. Long blasts on our siren to alert the next ship astern so that she can steer round it. When the ship ahead of us blasts her siren the order is 'Port or Starboard 10' to the helmsman to steer

Skipjack clear of the black blob, with its spiky horns sticking up all round it, looking like dirty fingers. These were the detonators and if anything broke one of them the mine would blow up. With great interest we watched it pass down our ship's side. This was minesweeping for real, sirens blowing from time to time and the odd explosion when a mine was blown up, its detonators activated by rifle shots from the ships' marksmen. Up and down, up and down the same old patch until we could guarantee the whole minefield had been laid to the correct depth. It was monotonous work but if we had not done our job meticulously a shallow mine could have sunk a cross channel ferry with heavy loss of life. The operation took several weeks.

Potentially, the act of minesweeping is dangerous. A minesweeper is actively searching for weapons that could destroy her, but which she seeks to destroy. In World War II we had applied the lessons of World War I and minesweeping was comparatively safe but it depends on three important human qualities: precision, alertness and cooperation.

In World War II the exact position of an enemy minefield was seldom known because mines were dropped by aircraft, laid by submarines or E-boats under cover of darkness. E-boats were fast patrol boats equipped with torpedoes or mines. The initial sweep for moored mines had to start outside the suspected area and then you worked towards the centre. Precise navigational fixes to determine the exact position of the minesweepers at all times were essential so that if a ship blew up the location of the minefield would be known. Even more important is the precision of keeping ships in a tight pre-determined formation while sweeping. Usually we swept in arrowhead formation where, except for the leading ship, the rest tucked in behind the far end of the sweep wire of the ship ahead. It was most important to keep within this protective zone and the Officer of the Watch needed to keep an eagle eye on the float ('dolphin') of the ship ahead and keep it on his outer bow. Then the ship was safe but he still had to keep a watchful eye for any surfaced mines cut by the ships ahead.

Precision is also essential at the back end of the ship when sweeps are being streamed or hauled in. The speed of letting out the wires or hauling them in needs to be carefully monitored. Too slow when streaming the sweeps and the wires trail along the seabed and tangle in rocks or wreckage. Too fast in hauling and the wire may part. Precision of speed control is vital.

Everyone concerned with the sweep must be constantly alert. The Officer of the Watch on the bridge must relentlessly watch the sweep of the ship ahead; at any moment a black balloon may burst out of the sea and soon it will be bouncing along towards you. Best to avoid it. At the back end of the ship the sweep deck officer and his crew must keep a close eye on their own sweep. If the sweep cuts a mine mooring the bridge must be told at once so that the siren can be sounded to warn the rest of the flotilla. Occasionally the sweep wire fails to cut the mine mooring and then the 'dolphin' may start performing strange fish-like manoeuvres, diving under the sea one minute and shooting into the air the next. The shout goes up 'mine in the sweep' and this requires a special drill by the Captain and Officer of the Watch to dislodge it, using speed and wheel alterations.

The time when an alert lookout is most essential, and it depends on one man the sweep deck officer, is when the sweep wires are being hauled in at the end of the sweep. Sometimes a mine becomes trapped in the end of the sweep wire after its mooring wire has been cut and it fails to surface. It lurks there unseen right at the end of the wire and it must be spotted before it blows the stern off the ship. Whenever a minesweeper is handling its sweeps everyone needs to be on maximum alert, including the engine room staff who have to respond rapidly to orders from the bridge for changes of speed. They are usually particularly alert as they would be major casualties if the ship blew up.

A most important piece of minesweeping safe practice is that human quality of close cooperation. This entails cooperation between three individuals: the Captain on the bridge looking aft to watch the sweep deck, the First Lieutenant watching the sweep wires and the Chief Stoker operating the two winches round which the sweep wires are wound.

Boredom was the only danger as the ships swept up and down the lines of mines and nothing happened hour after hour. Vigilance was likely to slip and then there would be an abrupt awakening as one of the ships ahead started blasting on her siren and that ugly black football came dancing towards you.

Only once did we nearly have to swim for our lives. A mine got jammed in our sweep wire near the end of it and as the wire was being wound in the mine drew closer to the stern unseen under the surface. Suddenly it appeared hanging below the stern some six feet from the ship. The First Lieutenant immediately stopped and reversed the direction of our sweep wire; the crowded quarterdeck was cleared and men evaporated in the opposite direction. On the bridge we slowly increased speed to put more distance between us and the horrible object. After the outbreak of war we became more used to these little dramas.

One day when we had been sweeping near the Goodwin Sands and were recovering our sweeps one of our flotilla was lifted by a huge explosion near her stern. Her sweep wires had set off a mine detonator beneath the surface of the sea. A split second later another explosion erupted and the little ship was hidden from sight by a huge column of water. '*Hussar*'s gone,' shouted my Captain as our sister ship disappeared in a wall of sea around her stern, but as he spoke *Hussar* appeared through the cascade of water unscathed. She had trapped two mines in her sweep wire and they had exploded near her stern.

It was one of our more exciting days. Half an hour later after we had retrieved our sweeps and were returning to harbour we sighted one of our anti-submarine sloops sailing into an area we had not yet checked. She was in danger and we flashed frantic signals at her to reverse her course.

'You are standing into danger. Reverse course immediately.'

Too late. An almighty explosion wrenched her amidships and her bows and stern sagged downwards into the sea. She lay paralysed and seemed about to sink.

'Away lifeboat's crew.'

'Sub,' said the Captain, 'take the whaler and stand by to pick up survivors.'

We rowed over to the helpless wreck but by the time we got there her Captain told me he thought she was stable and he had signalled for the rescue tug from Dover. In case she had to abandon ship *Skipjack* passed a towing wire to her and slowly we took her in tow until we were relieved some hours later by the rescue tug. Then we returned thankfully to harbour after a long and exhausting day when we were reminded that danger always lurked, even if we were not at war. The sloop eventually arrived safely in harbour but five of her crew were killed and several more injured. I believe the Captain was court-martialled.

Minesweeping in the Dover Straits was a pleasure for the navigator. The magnificent white cliffs of Dover backed by the green hills of the Downs with the towering might of Dover Castle made a beautiful backdrop and provided plenty of navigational marks to fix the ship's position. On fine days it was a joy to be at sea. The greatest navigational problem was the density of commercial shipping. A minesweeper with two long wires trailing 150 yards astern is not very manoeuvrable and all shipping was supposed to get out of her way but many failed to and panics stations ensued. We never had a crash but plenty of near misses.

We went on sweeping from sunrise to early evening and then popped in to Dover for a few hours every night. Occasionally we had two days off for maintenance and then there was time for a quick 'run ashore' and a walk along the cliffs.

August was coming to an end and summer was fading and so was the hope of peace. The international tension was unbearable. The British and French Governments ordered full mobilisation of all army, navy and air force reservists. The German army was massing on its eastern frontiers opposite Poland. It only needed a spark to set Europe alight again.

In the summer of 1939 our Government was negotiating with Russia to ensure her support if we were involved in a war with Germany. Nazi Germany and Russia had been bitter ideological enemies since Hitler came to power in 1933 and it seemed natural that Russia would be opposed to any further Nazi extensions of power, particularly to the east. So it was to Britain's astonishment and fury when Stalin and Hitler unexpectedly announced that they had made a non-aggression pact, which promised they would not attack each other. This gave Hitler the green light to go to war as he now knew his rear was secure. He had nothing to fear from Russia and the prize for the Soviets was that they were free to invade the eastern half of Poland – a neat carve-up for Hitler and Stalin but not for the wretched Poles. Russia eventually received her comeuppance when Hitler double-crossed her and, in flagrant disregard of their agreement, attacked Russia in the spring of 1941. Stalin and Hitler were both arch-shits and would qualify for a Nobel Prize for evil. Now we knew it could only be a matter of days before war came. It was like one of those nightmares where you are driving a car very fast and see another car coming towards you and you can't avoid it. In your dream you wake up but not in real life. All the slaughter of World War I seemed to have been in vain and the killing was going to happen all over again.

On the last day of August Hitler, without warning, invaded Poland. German aircraft bombed the cities and the airfields and the Poles appealed to the British and French to come to their aid. We had a treaty with Poland to come to her aid if she was attacked. It took four days for the democracies to react and declare war on Germany and in those four days Polish resistance was destroyed.

During those final months of peace we had been working so hard that there was no time to feel apprehensive about the future. We had accepted that World War II would break out before winter and there was no time to peer into the future and wonder what our fate would be. Rather we wanted to 'get on with it' and face whatever challenges war might bring.

It was all so different from only twelve months earlier when I was still longing for peace and hoping the war clouds would drift away; when I was hoping for any solution except having to fight. Then I was for appeasement and now I was a converted warrior.

Chapter Four

Excitement

War

On 3 September 1939 *Skipjack* was in Dover Harbour. There was a knock on my cabin door.

'Cipher for decoding, sir.' I was still half asleep.

'*Sir*, there is a signal for you to decode.'

By this time I was alert. The time was 6 am. I went to the office and got out the cipher books. 'TOTAL GERMANY 1100' was the decode. In plain language this meant 'War with Germany will start at 1100'. There was no time for histrionics. I alerted the Captain and other officers. Nothing more to be done. It had been expected. This was war and we were at the beginning of another ghastly bloodletting.

My mind raced. I was going to die. It would be a long and terrible struggle, but this time it was essential. We were fighting evil. No half heartedness now. This was a *just* war. We had to fight and get it over. All these somewhat incoherent thoughts tumbled out of my mind as I gazed out of the porthole at Dover's white cliffs.

Then with all this emotion boiling inside me I felt impelled to write to my mother and thank her for her love and her single-handed struggle to bring up her three sons. I felt sure I would be dead within a few weeks and this was a farewell letter. I believe this is a common reaction before battle. As my pen wavered over the pages self pity overcame me and tears poured down my cheeks and blotted out the writing, then my sense of the ridiculous rescued me and I told myself that this was no way to start a war and tore up the damp sheets of writing paper and went and had breakfast.

As 11.00 hours approached the Ship's Company sat glued to the radio and precisely at 11.00 the lugubrious voice of Neville Chamberlain, the Prime Minister, told us 'We are now at war with Germany'. We expected massive air raids to herald the start of the war. Huge underground shelters had been built in London and other large cities and everyone had been issued with gas masks.

Being based at Dover, the nearest UK port to the German air bases, we felt sure we would be singled out for an early bombing raid. How right we were. At 11.05 hours the air raid sirens started their banshee wailings.

'Air Raid Warning Red. Close Up At Action Stations,' was ordered over the tannoy.

Standing alongside 'A' gun I scanned the skies for the hostile hordes (no ship's radar in those days). It was a beautiful summer's day, with sunshine and blue skies with a few fluffy clouds skipping along overhead. My outstanding memory is of the seagulls screeching above the mast and diving into the water for scraps. Didn't they know there was a war on and we might be dead in a few minutes?

After half an hour the long clear note of the 'All Clear' told us death was postponed for now. Such was our relief that the officers repaired to the wardroom to stiffen their sinews with a few gins while the lower deck was issued with their usual noonday tot of rum. And that was the end of our first day of war. We felt a bit deflated: there had been no need to die for our country. We had faced the threat with sangfroid and determination. Rule Britannia.

After the razzmatazz of the declaration of war and the air raid warning and the false alarms I got on with my humdrum task of amending the navigation charts from the latest Admiralty corrections. Then when I turned in for the night I reflected on this strange day and two emotions jostled together in my mind. Elation and Apprehension. Elation that the tension of the last few months was over. The die was now cast and life ahead seemed simpler; war. There would be excitements and the thrills of battle. I felt a sense of history supporting me – the Armada and Trafalgar. It was our turn now. But there also lurked a sharper feeling of apprehension. There would be dangers and disasters to face. Would I show fear? How would I summon up the courage to face the enemy? Or would I crack? 'Could I stiffen the sinews and summon up the blood' (Henry V before the Battle of Agincourt). All these doubts and fears flashed through my mind, but I slept soundly at the end of that first day of World War II.

Those early weeks of the war were some of the most peculiar of my life. We had keyed ourselves up to expect mayhem and intense action and here we were in gorgeous weather steaming up and down the Channel in a calm sea with not a sign of the enemy. It was as peaceful as a quiet Sunday afternoon in the country. I revelled being at sea in those early weeks of the war, plotting the ship's position on the chart; giving orders to the helmsman in the wheelhouse on the deck below and chatting to the signalman on watch. Always keeping a good lookout for the expected enemy aircraft. At last I was putting into action all that I had been prepared for over the last seven years. It all seemed very deceptive; where was the war?

In the early weeks of the war I never had time for an evening 'run ashore' and apart from a trip to the bank to draw the cash for the fortnightly pay day I only once hit the beach. During one of our short maintenance breaks in harbour my whole family (Mother, brothers, aunt and cousins) drove over from Bexhill and we had what I felt was a farewell picnic on the cliffs above Dover Harbour looking across to the French coast. Being terribly British we did not speak our thoughts, but I am sure they had come to say goodbye in case they didn't see me again.

The only mildly exciting event was the passage of the troop ships carrying the British Army, known as the British Expeditionary Force, to France and Belgium. Our job was to sweep the passage routes and make sure they were mine-free. There was not a single casualty during the crossing.

At this time an air of unreality enclosed us and the earlier apprehensions when war broke out became submerged and forgotten. From being concerned whether or not I should be able to hide my fears there was a happy acceptance that war was rather enjoyable. Hard work, quiet contentment at being on top of my job and lovely coastal scenery made seagoing a delight. War had become normal, routine. Yet there was a niggle that something was wrong with this rosy scenario. We were soon to find out.

Before war broke out we started sweeping the convoy lanes to keep them clear of mines. All the way round the coasts of Britain shipping lanes had been set up through which all merchant ships were routed and they had to sail in convoy. These lanes were repeatedly swept by flotillas of minesweepers and our patch ran from Dover to the Humber. One glorious sunny day in October 1939 we were sweeping off the Essex coast. I was lounging in the warm sunshine, perched on the wing of the ship's bridge, with little to do but watch the 'dolphin' marking the end of the sweep wire of the ship ahead and keep an eye on our own sweep. If the 'dolphin' of the ship ahead dipped under the sea a mine might pop up at any minute, looking rather like a plum pudding and I would have to avoid it and summon the Captain.

Behind us a huge convoy stretched out of sight to the north, bringing precious supplies to London Docks, then one of the busiest unloading ports in the UK. Oil from the Middle East, munitions from America, food from Australia, New Zealand and Africa: all desperately needed in besieged Britain. Our job was to see the ships safely home and they were very nearly there. It was always immensely satisfying to think we played some part in their safe arrival.

Nothing had happened all morning, not a mine in sight, and I was quietly enjoying the peacefulness of the scene. The usually cold, grey North Sea was dancing like quick silver under the hot sun. There was hardly a cloud in a light blue sky, which turned green as it merged with the sea at the far horizon. The great ships in convoy astern of us ploughed serenely on.

Suddenly, there was a mighty clap of thunder astern of us. It was not thunder – a large cargo vessel quickly settled down by the bows and some minutes later the sea engulfed her. What had happened? No enemy aircraft or submarines had been detected. Had we failed to sweep the convoy's channel clear of mines?

The convoy steamed on, avoiding the sinking ship. Twenty minutes later there was another loud *boom* and a sheet of flame soared skywards as a tanker blew up, turning into a fiery furnace, which was not extinguished until she exploded and her remains sank sizzling under the waves. The idyllic day had turned into a nightmare.

Being the navigator I checked again the area we were supposed to have cleared of mines. The flotilla had covered every inch of the channel through which the convoy was sailing and it should have been mine-free. Then yet another explosion rent the air and a third ship heeled over to port as if she might capsize. What had gone so terribly wrong?

A few weeks later we got the answer. This was one of the first attacks by the new German magnetic mines, which lay on the seabed and exploded when the magnetic field from a ship's steel hull passed over them and activated the detonators. These mines needed no wire to moor them as they did not need to strike the ship's bottom. Our sweeps were only designed to cut the wires of mines moored to the seabed and were useless against these new magnetic mines.

Seeing these huge vessels being destroyed made me think about the merchant seamen who sailed in them. They couldn't fight back and the ships in convoy just had to plod on while ships sank around them. During the war some merchant seamen survived three sinkings and many had no grave but the sea. Yet they went on going to sea to bring the country all that was needed for its survival. Few now remember that 97% of all our requirements in World War II had to be brought in by sea. Had these men failed the war would have been lost.

I came across a haunting poem by an RAF radar operator, Molly Repard, who had obviously lost a lover at sea who had no known grave.

> You who know not where your lover died–
> Search where the wind blows free
> the hundred thousand miles of open sea
> and weep your longing out to every tide.

This was the beginning of a dark period in our little war. Some brilliant brain on the staff ashore decided that fleet minesweepers had too small a magnetic field to set off a magnetic mine and that if they towed their sweep wires just above the seabed they might blow up the new mines astern of them. For a few days we were set the task of trying to locate these magnetic mines and detonating them with our sweeps. We, at sea, knew this was lunacy as we were quite large enough to set off a mine and our sweep wires had too small a magnetic field to blow one up. During this crazy exercise I remained on the bridge expecting to be propelled skywards at any time. Then there was always a hope that one might plop safely into the ocean and be picked up.

Fortunately, one of the new mines was discovered on the mud flats in the Thames Estuary and Lieutenant-Commander Ouvry, a mine specialist, volunteered to try and dismantle it and reveal its secrets. As he took it apart he gave a running commentary to his No. 2, a Chief Petty Officer, who was stationed some distance away so that he would survive if the mine blew up and would be able to report back. Ouvry was successful and the scientists rapidly designed countermeasures. For this calm and deliberate act of bravery Ouvry was awarded the George Cross, the highest bravery award for 'conduct not in the face of the enemy' and equivalent to the Victoria Cross.

After some hair-raising days we stopped trying to sweep magnetic mines with wire sweeps. Specialised trawlers, whose hulls were demagnetised, became the work horses for magnetic mine clearance, towing astern of them a huge magnetised coil that blew up the mines. Apart from this frisson of excitement over magnetic mines the war bumbled on and nothing much happened. It was almost boring.

Then came the first wartime Christmas and luckily the ship was in dock for minor repairs. I was given leave to go home to Bexhill-on-Sea where we had an extraordinary Christmas. Many of my family were there: the war was hardly mentioned. It seemed thousands of miles away. All the traditional customs were observed: carol singing, turkey and plum pudding, games and the usual Christmas tree laden with presents. It might have been the piping days of peace with all thought of the war forgotten. Such interludes during the war left me a touch uneasy.

I was soon back to reality as the flotilla was ordered north to Scapa Flow, the main British fleet naval base in the Orkney Islands. The land war became known as the phoney war because nothing happened. On one side the French and British armies were lined up along the fortifications called the Maginot Line with the German army opposite them. No one blinked. But the war at sea was hotting up. There were attacks on merchant shipping by U-boats, armed raiders on the far off oceans and occasional air raids on naval bases and minelaying along the east coast, but it was still small beer.

Scapa Flow, in the Orkney Islands, is a large inland waterway with many channels into the Flow, girdled by many islands, sparsely inhabited, except for the main island, quaintly called Mainland, which is actually some twenty miles away in Scotland. These channels had all been blocked by sunken blockships and anti-submarine boom nets, or so everyone thought. Scapa Flow was the main naval base for our huge Home Fleet and was considered impregnable.

An enterprising U-boat commander, Lieutenant-Commander Prien, had spent time submerged, checking the entrances and had discovered one where the position of the block ship had shifted and by deft manoeuvring he found a route into the main fleet anchorage. At 01.04 hours on 14 October 1939 Prien found HMS *Royal Oak*, where I had spent over two years as a midshipman, at anchor. The official Admiralty report states that 'It was a fine clear night, the sea was calm and the sky lit up by the Northern Lights'. Prien fired his first salvo of torpedoes at close range and hit the battleship near her bows. So certain were the officers on board that no submarine could get into the Flow that they thought the ship had suffered an internal explosion, possibly in a magazine. In such a safe anchorage the crew were relaxed and most were asleep and not much disturbed by the first explosion. Twelve minutes later there were three shattering explosions as Prien made his second attack and this had a catastrophic effect. The great ship heeled rapidly over to starboard and capsized at 01.29 hours.

The Ship's Company, many still asleep, did not have much chance to escape and 853 drowned that night. When I heard what had happened I thought of the many young midshipmen and officers I had known. It was an appalling shock but we were busy sweeping mines and life had to go on. There is no time for sentimentality in war.

Scapa Flow is a bleak sheet of sea intersected by equally bleak little islands, mostly heather covered, but some ran sheep. The anchorage for the minesweepers was between the islands of Hoy and Flotta. Except for a NAAFI Club for the ratings in a large shed near Lyness there was no social life ashore. When we were in harbour a few intrepid sailors would land and imbibe huge quantities of lukewarm beer, but there was no outlet for the officers except to drink on board. Some took to the booze but were able to recover as we never drank at sea. In harbour, life was comfortable; we had three reasonable meals a day with a hot bath in the evening if you wanted it. What more could one want but it was desperately dull.

Our main enemy was the winter weather and the long, dark northern nights. Ferocious winds swept through the anchorage and ships had to raise steam so that their engines could be worked to prevent them being blown on to the beach. Miserably cold nights were spent on the bridge to ensure our anchors were not dragging and losing their hold.

Our minesweeping task was to sweep the main channel for the Home Fleet when it left harbour and also to keep the convoy channel round the north and east coasts of Scotland clear of mines. Long hours at sea and the intense work of navigation helped to pass the dark winter months. The stormy seas and winds were more of an enemy than the Germans. Looking back, the winter of 1939/1940 was a strange interlude; the land war had not started; there was little naval action in the North Sea and we never felt threatened when we went about our daily minesweeping. My job interested me and I got to know and like our seamen, with whom I had a good relationship, as close as officers and men could enjoy in those class conscious days. The Ship's Company had become a 100%

efficient minesweeping crew with a remarkable sense of black humour, which they needed as life was basic when we were minesweeping.

To minimise casualties if we were blown up all the spaces below the waterline were battened down whenever our sweeps were streamed. What were called 'minesweeping messes' had to be used on the upper deck behind canvas screens and they were draughty and uncomfortable. Here the denizens of the lower messdecks ate their meals whilst the northern winds whistled round their feet.

After six months of war I was confident that I had the navigating job taped. Possibly a bit overconfident. We had spent many weeks sailing along the east coast between Dover and the Humber, sometimes on our own, where there are nests of sandbanks, which can grab the unwary as can be seen by the hundreds of wrecks marked on the charts. We had also skirted the ferocious cliffs and rocks off the northern Scottish coast so I suffered a severe blow to my pride one evening when we were approaching Peterhead on the north-east Scottish coast. My only excuse was that there was a thick fog and our only navigational aid was a seaman with a sounding line with which he checked the depth of the water as we steamed slowly towards the harbour entrance between two breakwaters. We still had no radar. We could just about see fifty yards ahead as we edged cautiously towards the land. Suddenly I heard a train's whistle as it was leaving the station. I had noticed earlier that the station was right alongside the beach.

'Full speed astern, sir'? to the Captain, 'Beach ahead.'

'Yes.'

'Coxswain emergency full speed astern.'

As we slowed and gathered sternway the ripple of waves breaking on the sand could just be seen. Would we go aground? Even in wartime putting your ship ashore was a court martial offence for the Captain and navigator. Slowly the ship gathered her speed astern and there were no nasty little bumps under the ship's bottom. We were clear, but it was a black mark for the navigator. When the fog cleared in the morning we were less than 100 yards from the entrance, but we had had to anchor in the open sea, not an enjoyable pastime as we would be a sitting duck for a submarine.

This was our life; to sea every day in the grey dawn; out sweeps when we reached the convoy route; ploughing up and down all the mercifully short winter daylight hours and into the nearest harbour for the rest of the night. That winter was blisteringly cold and I used to wear pyjama trousers under my uniform to keep the nether parts from freezing.

The only compensating factor was the magnificence of the coastal scenery. Surely the north coast of Scotland must be the finest in the British Isles. The towering black cliffs soaring up into the sky with the storm-tossed waves crashing on to the rocks below were a marvel to watch as we steamed along from Duncansby Head to Cape Wrath.

Came March and the beginning of the end of a long, dark winter. *Skipjack* was sent to Aberdeen for her periodical maintenance, known as the 'boiler clean' because the boilers that provided the steam that drove the engines had to be descaled or, like a kettle, they could get furred up. As we entered harbour it was so cold there were ice flows floating around in the inner harbour and we had to navigate with great care.

By a fluke of good fortune the dates of our boiler clean coincided with my Coming of Age – I was twenty-one on 13 March 1940.

'Three days' leave, Tony,' said my Captain. 'No need for a navigator in harbour.'

I was off like a pellet out of a catapult, but could I get home and back and celebrate my Coming of Age all within three days? Home at that time was Belstone on Dartmoor in far away Devon. It was worth a go. I rushed to the station and caught the night train to London, packed full of sailors going on leave from the Home Fleet. Seats had to be shared as well as bottles of beer. The mood was buoyant and the carriages filled with song. Away from the war, cast cares aside and let rip.

Bleary eyed we baled out at St Pancras dead on time and I dashed across London to Waterloo Station to catch the Okehampton train. There was just time to ring home to see if the one village taxi had enough petrol to meet me. I was home in time for lunch.

Now what about the big party? I found my mother was all alone. My brothers were away at boarding school; village friends, including all the girls, had been conscripted, not quite the setting for the wild orgy that I had pictured.

However, the next day Dartmoor looked beautiful under a clear blue sky. The great hills spoke of eternal peace and obliterated the horrors and strains of war. Yes, it was worth coming all this way just for that. My mother and I took a picnic lunch up on to the moor, miles from any civilisation, and celebrated my twenty-first birthday beside a stream, the Brim Brook, below the highest point on Dartmoor, the High Willhays. I was now the heir to the McCrum fortunes, which turned out to be one silver cigarette box some thirty years later. I don't smoke. Whenever I walked down the Brim Brook, sixty years later, I thought of the elaborate celebrations for our sons' twenty-firsts. Tables groaning with food, champagne, music, girls, dancing into the night. Am I envious? You bet I am, but it wasn't a bad day with a lovely walk and the war thousands of miles away.

The next day I caught the train back to Aberdeen. When my fellow officers heard my story they took me for a 'run ashore' and 'we let go the end', a nautical term derived from the moment when a team of sailors have been heaving on a rope with a heavy load on the end and have finally got the load on board. Then thankfully they drop the rope and 'let go the end'. Now it means having a great party when everyone will let go the end and celebrate *ssshplendidly* – an earlier version of binge drinking.

We were soon back to the daily grind up and down the convoy lanes or the Fleet exit channels. Seldom did we find a mine and the daily chore of a dawn departure from Scapa was becoming monotonous. This wasn't war: there was no excitement, each day being the same as the day before. Of course it didn't last. In April we were ordered south to Dover where we had started the war. In May the German armies overran Holland and Belgium. Merciless mass bombing of major cities like Amsterdam cowed the civilian population and the Dutch and Belgian armies put up a hopeless fight against the magnificently efficient German army and irresistible *Luftwaffe*.

On the East Coast where we were sweeping the convoy routes into the Thames we watched helplessly as ships and boats of every description were fleeing from the Dutch coast to the safety of Yarmouth, Lowestoft and other east coast ports. A British destroyer managed to embark the Dutch Queen Wilhelmina and her family just in time before German soldiers overran the royal palace.

I don't remember feeling scared or depressed or even worried. We were too busy with our own little minesweeping war and the spring hours of daylight meant many hours on the bridge with only a few hours' rest in harbour at night. The rest was brief as there were still the charts to be kept corrected up to date. Accurate corrections are critical in wartime because so many ships are sunk by aircraft or mines and their skeletons lie on the seabed, a danger to our sweep wires.

We had come to accept war as the normal state of affairs. It no longer seemed unusual and fears had been banished to the back burner. Less than twelve months before when war broke out I was in fear; fear of showing fear. Would I disgrace myself? Now I felt a certain numbness, a suppression of such emotions. They didn't bother me any more. Later when fear did come, as it did at Dunkirk, it did not overcome me. This was war: this was what we expected and we kept all our feelings buttoned up; fear and sadness at the loss of friends controlled.

Apprehension is a more insidious emotion. As President Roosevelt memorably exclaimed 'We have nothing to fear except fear'. Certainly at the start of the struggle I was morbidly apprehensive. I imagined scenes of destruction, of being maimed, losing both legs, my eyesight. My conceptions of fighting were grounded in the stories of the dreadful slaughter of World War I and the heavy casualties inflicted on that war's minesweepers, blown up by German mines. How would I cope? Then these apprehensions quickly died away as our sea war became part of our every day life.

Most days it was a pleasure to be at sea steaming along against the backdrop of the magnificent cliffs of northern Scotland or the gentler white cliffs of Dover. When the sun shone and the sea on the far horizon danced against the sky it was a joy to be alive. I was always entranced by the patterns of cloud, sky and sea, ever changing to reflect wind and weather. Even a storm has its own grandeur as the breakers tower over the bridge and come crashing down on the foc'sle and the ship shudders but drives on through the green wall of sea.

In a few months we had gone from this apprehensive fear to a quiet acceptance that war was mostly routine with few excitements and the absorption of doing a worthwhile job sweeping mines and comparatively happy seagoing days contributing to a successful war effort and eventual victory. Thus when the spectre of terror stalked amongst us at Dunkirk, and occasionally when sweeping, it was just a blip on our mostly peaceful operations. We could take it in our stride because we knew it wouldn't last.

There was one fear that never assailed me – drowning. I never visualised myself drowning and hardly ever thought about it and when I did it didn't bother me. I was far more concerned that I might suffer appalling wounds, physical or mental, which would destroy my life. The thought that I might live for fifty years as a human wreck worried me far more than the extinction of death. This was brought home to me one day when we had an RAF pilot, about my age, on board for a day at sea to observe our operations as he flew Spitfires, which patrolled the convoy routes to protect us from enemy air attack. We got to discussing how we faced danger.

'I could never do what you're doing; the thought of being blown up and drowning fills me with horror,' said the pilot.

'Well,' I said, 'the thought that I might be trapped in a cockpit plunging to earth would be a nightmare I would never be capable of facing.'

After that we called it quits and talked of pleasant things like girl friends.

Each day had the same pattern. As soon as we got back into harbour after the day's sweep we had a quick supper, a stint correcting charts, and then the most unpleasant task of censoring the Ship's Company letters to see if there were any breaches of security. This was much resented by the Ship's Company and hated by the censoring officers. Each evening all the outgoing letters were brought to the wardroom and the officers foregathered and shared them out. If in doubt about security we consulted each other, otherwise strict confidentiality was maintained. If a breach was spotted the passage had to be cut out with a pair of scissors and some letters ended up looking like a lace mat. One of the difficulties was that we were not allowed to inform the culprit.

As a very young innocent officer I found some letters quite educational. There was one splendid husband who, deprived of his connubial delights, described in precise and lurid details what he would like to be doing if he was in bed with his wife. Then there was a young fresh-faced youth of seventeen years who wrote reams to his beloved granny who had brought him up. He came from the Tyneside and had an extensive range of invective to describe his life on board. He invariably started his letters: 'Dear Nan, You give me the fucking shits' and then he would explain why she had earned this opprobrium. Usually she had forgotten to send him some sweets or a cake. But mostly the letters were brief and boring, probably because they knew they were being read by their officers.

Although we hardly noticed it the land war was heading for disaster. The German *blitzkrieg* steamrollered through Holland and Belgium and the British Expeditionary Force made gallant attempts to halt the Nazi advance but without much effect. All along the western front the Germans seemed unstoppable. Looking back it is strange how unaffected we were by all the gloom ashore. We just went on sweeping. Until one day we were ordered to carry out a special operation – excitement at last.

As the German army swept into Belgium their coastal ports were about to fall into enemy hands. Zeebrugge, a port on the Belgian coast, had to be blocked before the Germans overran it so that the enemy E-boats could not use it. In World War I there had been a famous raid on Zeebrugge when we effected a similar blockade but then the harbour was in German hands. Now we just held it, but it was expected to fall at any time. Our flotilla was to sweep a passage across the Channel to ensure the blockships arrived safely after dark and also to act as their escorts. It was a moonlit night and as the convoy approached the port enemy bombers started a night attack on the blockships and on us. Without radar our first intimation of the attack was bombs exploding in the sea close to our bows. Luckily the enemy didn't have radar either. Accurate bombing by night in those days was difficult but it was even more impossible for us to fire at the small targets of the aircraft as they swooped down on us.

We had no idea of the number of enemy aircraft or of their height and we could not see them at all until suddenly a black shadow, like a large bat, flew over us and was gone in a few seconds. There was nothing we could do. There is nothing worse in war than being under attack and not being able to fight back. Action gets all the adrenalin flowing and drives away fear. The gun crews were ordered to lie flat on the deck with their heads inboard to lessen the danger of splinter wounds from 'near misses' exploding in the sea. I was hopelessly trying to control the forward gun and lay down with the crew trying to conjure up memories of happy occasions to ward off my fears.

For what seemed like an hour, but was probably only twenty minutes, we lay like corpses and every now and again we saw these black phantoms sweeping across us and then a huge explosion somewhere near. They never hit us but this brief episode was one of my most terrifying of the whole war. That night my morale hit rock bottom and I remember thinking 'Let's go back; let's go back; bugger the blockships'. Afterwards I was much ashamed of myself. The blockships were sunk across the entrances and the operation was a success and we returned to harbour undamaged.

This was a foretaste of a much more exciting event, the evacuation of the British Expeditionary Force from Dunkirk, which took place a few weeks later.

Chapter Five

Too Much Excitement

Dunkirk

Being based at Dover, only twenty-five miles from the French and Belgian coasts, we were amongst the first ships to bring our soldiers off the beaches at Dunkirk. This was one of the few occasions during the war when I wrote a contemporary account of my experiences. Reading them again nearly seventy years later they make me blush as they are somewhat excitable and naïve but my story accurately reflects what I had felt at the time and I think it is worth recording. In war the fighting man thinks what he sees is also happening everywhere else when, in fact, he only glimpses a small segment of the battle scene and his experiences are only a tiny snapshot of a much bigger panorama.

So when my account rails against the lack of organisation on the Dunkirk beaches in the early days I knew nothing of the Herculean efforts being made by Captain Tennant and the naval beach parties to bring order out of chaos. When we first arrived off the beaches on 28 May 1940 there was no beach organisation to direct our boats ferrying soldiers out to the waiting ships, but they were established by the time of our second trip. Sometimes the beach parties were overwhelmed by the sheer number of soldiers waiting to be evacuated and by some indiscipline in the early days. It was noticeable that the front-line troops maintained an immaculate discipline throughout but occasionally, there was some trouble loading the boats with men from some of the support units. Others have written of confusion and chaos on the beaches, but the fact that over 400,000 British *and* French soldiers were lifted off open beaches and the mole in Dunkirk Harbour surely shows that this was a fantastically successful, even miraculous, event.

Another total misconception that arose amongst us sailors and soldiers was that the RAF was doing nothing to protect us. As the bombs crashed into ships and on to the beaches the cry went up 'Where's the RAF? Where's the RAF?' In our ignorance we imagined lots of Hurricanes and Spitfires flying overhead shooting down the *Stukas* (dive-bombers). When we became more savvy we knew that friendly fighters have to be deployed a long way from the enemy's target area so that their bombers can be shot down before they reach their targets. Many *Stukas* were shot down before they got to Dunkirk but sheer numbers overwhelmed our defences. With hindsight it would have helped morale if we had been told how the RAF was fighting and how many aircraft they were destroying as was done later in the Battle of Britain.

Despite my more mature understanding of the events at Dunkirk I will let my comments, written soon after the heat of battle, stand. This is what I thought and felt at the time at the age of twenty-one.

On 28th May 1940 *Skipjack* left her anchorage in the Downs near Dover to carry out routine minesweeping in the Dover Straits. About 4.30 pm as we were preparing to return to Dover a signal was received to 'proceed to a beach near the Belgian seaside resort of La Panne'. *Skipjack* was with *Halcyon*, *Salamander*, *Fitzroy* and *Sutton* (all Dover minesweepers) and we proceeded in company until we were approaching the coast when each ship operated independently to get as close as possible to the beach.

All we knew was that we had to contact some army officers who would give us further information. We had no idea that we were the vanguard of what turned out to be a huge evacuation. We were the very first ships to evacuate our soldiers. The coastline along the Belgian shore is flat; the sea is shallow and there are many sandbanks. During the war nearly all lighthouses, lightships and light buoys were extinguished, which made night navigation difficult. There were no lights to guide the ship and it was essential this evening to bring the ship as close as possible to the shore without grounding, so we slowed down and crept forwards, sounding the depth continuously.

'Five fathoms,' called the leadsman (a fathom is six feet so that meant we were in thirty feet of water).

'Deep four,' he cried again. We dare not go much further.

The Captain orders 'Stop both engines' and then 'Stand by to let go the port anchor'.

The cable rattles out; the navigator breathes a sigh of relief and the ship is in position as near the shore as possible. *Skipjack* draws ten feet of water and at low tide there will only be three feet under her keel. One man stands by and tests the depth of water every half hour for safety

Meanwhile as we were crawling up to our anchorage we could see dark shadows showing up against the white sand dunes like some huge black beetle spread across the beach. Hundreds of soldiers were waiting for us. To our great relief there was no sign of the enemy so we relaxed our precautions and sent our boats in to load up.

Young sailor. Tony's
first day in the Navy.
September 1932.

The Royal Naval College at Dartmouth above the River Dart.

1934. Drake Term march past the Prince of Wales, later King Edward VIII
who abdicated the throne.

Drake Term in front of the College in 1934. Tony is No 2 in the second seated row.

Alpha Class at Dartmouth in 1935.
Tony is No 2 in the back row.

Off to sea. Tony's first ship HMS *Frobisher* in 1936.

HMS *Royal Oak*. Midshipman training 1936-1939.

HMS *Basilisk*. Destroyer training for midshipmen.

The battleships of the Home Fleet in 1937, *Royal Oak* leading.

HMS *Skipjack*'s officers on the outbreak of war in 1939. Captain, First Lieutenant, Sub (Tony) and Chiefie, Engineer Officer.

Fleet Minesweeper, HMS *Skipjack*, sunk at Dunkirk, 1st June 1940.

Crew of HMS *Skipjack*.
19 drowned on
1st June 1940.

Sunken ships in Dunkirk harbour in June 1940.

Anti-aircraft gunner at action stations aboard HMS *Bridlington*.

Above and Below: Fleet Minesweeper HMS *Bridlington* at sea.

Officers of HMS *Bridlington*. First Lieutenant (Tony), Captain, Chiefie, Sub Lieutenant Davies, and seated, Sub

HMS *Bridlington*'s forward gun.

'Out Sweeps'. HMS *Bridlington*'s minesweeping quarterdeck as sweeps are 'streamed'.

'In Sweeps'. The float (dolphin) being recovered at the end of a day's minesweeping.

Off home, back to base at the end of the day.

Gun crew at drill, HMS *Bridlington*.

The Victory Parade through Toulon in 1944. It was led by two of my team, Telegraphist Beavan with the colour and Signalman Bivens as Escort. Beavan was a London policeman in peacetime.

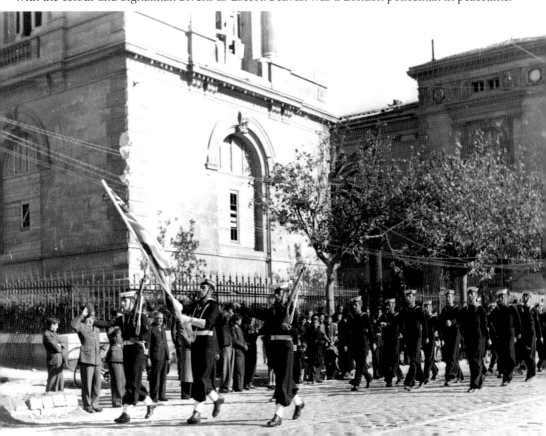

Three sailor brothers in December 1944 at Belstone on Dartmoor. Sub Lieutenant Michael, Lieutenant Tony and Cadet Robert.

Tribal Class destroyer HMS *Tartar* in the Bay of Bengal in 1945.

The first boat off brought a staff officer direct from Lord Gort's headquarters; Lord Gort was the General Officer Commanding the British Expeditionary Force. This officer immediately asked to see the Captain. He was very worried by the lack of organisation and cooperation and only then did we realise that the whole British Expeditionary Force was awaiting evacuation. At that early stage there were no naval beach parties to control the loading of boats, no piers and no pontoons. There were no small craft for ferrying duties except for the ship's own boats and no organisation at all. [Subsequent note: the naval beach operation had only just started.]

It was a flat sandy beach backed by grass-covered sand dunes about thirty feet high and ships' boats approaching the shore ran aground a long way to seaward and the slight surf rendered boat handling very difficult. The soldiers, weary after sleepless nights and fighting, struggled through the surf weighed down by their greatcoats and packs and had to be hauled into the boats. Hour after hour this tedious operation dragged on at the rate of an evacuation of about fifty men an hour.

By 3 am the first glimmer of dawn appeared and with it the grim reminder of enemy bombers. By 3.30 it was daylight and we were filling up gradually. The motor boat had broken down and each party of soldiers had to be rowed out to the ship. At long last at 4.30 we were full and had 180 men on board. With a joyful sense of relief we set off for home, for the long night had told on our nerves and we were glad to be speeding along, free to manoeuvre ever further away from enemy aircraft.

Our journey back to Dover was uneventful except for fresh evidence of the enemy's activities; the bows of a sunken British destroyer still showing above water, where she had been torpedoed by an enemy submarine only twelve hours before and a little further on we came on a German submarine being destroyed by the depth charges of Polish and British destroyers. As we steamed past we watched the slim grey form of the shattered submarine roll slowly over and slip beneath the sunlit sea. I for one could not help feeling sorry for the wretched men inside her. We disembarked our soldiers at Dover, had a few hours' rest and steamed back to the Belgian coast.

It was now 30 May and this time our embarkation point was Bray, the small resort some four miles east of Dunkirk where thousands of troops overflowed the beaches, waiting patiently for hours, even days, without food or sleep. Here, except for the distant rumble from Dunkirk, it was as peaceful as Brighton beach on an August evening. Boats were plentiful. A long pontoon of derelict lorries had been run out into the sea at low tide and the shore organisation rendered the embarkation swift and efficient. Within three hours we were once more on our way back to England. All we saw of the enemy were two German bombers away astern of us unloading their racks at random into the sea. The sun was shining and it was good to be alive. We had embarked 230 soldiers. On arrival at Dover we carried out the same routine.

Two hours' respite and then we were off once more. This time we reached Dunkirk earlier. The calm of summer twilight still lay over the beaches and nowhere was there any sign of the enemy. By 3 am 450 troops had been embarked and for the third time we left the white sands of France for the white cliffs of Dover. This was by far our best night and we reached Dover at 7 am on 31 May and were told we would not be required again until 6 pm that evening. I tumbled straight into my bunk for the first time since Monday (four days ago).

After four days' evacuation the ship was a shambles. Soldiers' gear littered every space, as well as scraps of food, dirty clothes and cigarette ends. We had no boats, having been ordered to leave them over the other side to assist the ferrying from shore to ship. In the afternoon came our final orders telling us that our flotilla of minesweepers would remove the last remnants of the army that night.

In a way it was a relief to feel that our task was almost fulfilled and we were proud that it had fallen to us, who had also been in at the beginning, but the best plans miscarry. Evidently the day's evacuation had not been as rapid as expected because on our way across the Channel our orders were changed and our final trip was postponed to the following day, but we still had our routine load for that day to take home. [Subsequent note: At the time of writing I only knew half the story. In fact, the destroyers embarking troops from the harbour mole were taking off far greater loads and it was decided to continue the evacuation to take off thousands of French troops.]

We arrived off La Panne at midnight only to find out that the shore organisation had broken down. It was low water and many boats lay stranded on the shore and we had none of our own as we had left them behind earlier to boost the number of boats available for the evacuation. The situation looked desperate as the enemy brought up some big guns and was shelling the beaches. Overhead enemy aircraft were dropping flares along the beaches to help their gunners as well as laying mines in the shipping lanes. Luckily the night was dark and the fires caused by the shelling were not enough to reveal us, but to our weary and stretched nerves, the unceasing sound of the shells crashing into La Panne was unbearable. Try as one might one could not be free of the din, which seemed to echo and resound inside one's very being. All the while we were snatching no soldiers from the beaches. We therefore decided to abandon our allotted positions and steam slowly towards Dunkirk but still we found no boats. Daybreak showed us that the mass of soldiers had moved to the west so we steamed to Bray where we knew there were boats. All the time the German artillery was creeping along the sands and the order was given for everyone to march towards Dunkirk. We reached Bray and soon began to fill up with tired soldiers. At about 6 am enemy aircraft put in an appearance, some twenty Messerschmitt 109s. They are dive-bombers. To our selfish relief they concentrated on the mole in Dunkirk Harbour. For an hour, it seemed more like ten hours, these attacks went on intermittently and when we opened fire with our 4-inch guns we did some good shooting, but these attacks slowed up the loading of troops. Then for a short space the skies cleared and we breathed again and prepared for a fresh onslaught. This soon came. At 8 am the skies above us darkened once more and the whole sky throbbed with the growl of hordes of aircraft, not ours. We kept our guns firing at top speed and began to gather headway to gain manoeuvring space to avoid the cascade of bombs.

Firstly, the enemy aimed at a destroyer a thousand yards away and missed her. Remorselessly they came round again and this time hit her four square. She did not sink but lay crippled at their mercy. Inexorably the bombers dived again on the doomed destroyer. This was too much for her and she sank slowly to the bottom, still remaining upright, like some stately old lady, while her sister ship went alongside her to take off survivors.

Then for a few minutes there was silence once more and the sky was free of the enemy. We stopped and waited for our last boatload of soldiers. Our ammunition was almost exhausted, as were the gun crews. These minutes of waiting were like hours; our nerves were as taut as violin strings. It was a great relief to haul the final boat load alongside. In a few minutes we would be on our way home again for the fourth time, away from the incessant din of battle and cries for help. Speeding along and slicing the white foam as we tore towards the white Dover cliffs. Thus it was in my imagination.

Nearly all the soldiers had clambered out of that last boat when suddenly another attack developed, this time on a destroyer and a gunboat off the harbour entrance. Hurriedly we cast off the boat and started for home at the same instant as half a dozen *Stukas* came down on us. The attack never developed and they dropped their bombs harmlessly into the sea two hundred yards away. By then we decided we had enough soldiers on board, some three hundred, and felt ready to be off.

Then we remembered that we had left a few of our own crew in a ferry launch and turned back to pick them up. As we did so ten *Stukas* swept out of the clouds in one straight line and hurtled down on us. The bridge shuddered and sparks of flame spurted from the deck and a loud report showed we had been hit at last. I rushed to the after end of the bridge to see the upper deck bend and crack as the ship broke her back. The engines had stopped. The guns were all out of action. I tried shouting to the forward gun just below the bridge, 'Keep on firing: keep on firing', not realising it had been hit by a bomb and the crew were dead or wounded. We were in the hands of our enemy. Then I realised we were in danger of sinking in the exit channel from the beaches out to the open sea. I called down to the Coxswain in the wheelhouse below 'Hard a port' to try and clear us out of the channel.

His voice came up the voicepipe 'Ship not answering her helm, sir.' I then knew that the steering gear had been smashed and we could not manoeuvre.

To my horror I saw seven more *Stukas* hurtling down on us. They were so close I could see the pilots' black helmets and I watched the bomb bay doors opening and what looked like black lozenges emerging rather slowly – the stick of bombs. One of them seemed to be aimed directly at the pit of my stomach. Instinctively, I crouched in the corner of the bridge and watched it getting closer and closer until it hit the bridge about ten feet from me, but it didn't explode. It penetrated two or three decks down and went off below. As it passed through the bridge the deck shuddered, acrid smoke enveloped me and tongues of flame licked the paintwork. I seemed to be alone. Where was the Captain? Where were the rest of the bridge crew? Were they all dead? I felt very isolated and lonely. Unharmed, I struggled clear of the smoke and flames and jumped down to the deck below. By this time the ship had rolled over so far that the normally vertical ship's side was now a gentle slope into the sea, down which men were walking calmly and carefully. I joined them and swam away as far as I could to avoid the down suction as the ship sank.

Turning on my back to watch her sink I saw the Captain emerge from the upper control position, which has emergency internal communications and is armour plated against machine-gun bullets. He had probably been trying to establish what damage the ship had suffered. He was the last to leave the ship. Then I had a nasty feeling that I should have waited on board for the order 'Abandon ship', although it is unlikely that such an order was possible. All communications had been cut by the first attack and the bridge had become untenable and everyone was walking over the side and I followed. I know the Captain survived but I never saw him again. He wrote that he had recommended me for a decoration but quite rightly Churchill ordered 'No medals for Dunkirk. Medals are not appropriate for a military disaster' and no Dunkirk medal has ever been produced.

The only medals for service in the evacuation that were approved were for acts of great personal bravery, such as the Distinguished Service Medal awarded to our Leading Seaman Macleod from Stornoway who manned the anti-aircraft machine-gun above the bridge. He shot down one confirmed enemy aircraft and went on reloading and firing until the sea lapped his feet. He got away. He was our only medallist.

There was a roar of many explosions and that almost human groaning that fractured steel makes and the ship heeled over for the last time. It was a lovely day for a bathe. Hot June sunshine and a sandy beach a few hundred yards away, but the enemy continued his attacks on the survivors in the water. The sea was swarming with swimmers. We were not the only ship sunk that morning. The saddest memory was hearing soldiers crying 'Help' as they had no lifejackets. We all tried to help each other but it was a scene of chaos and many drowned.

My first feeling had been one of exhilaration. I had my lifejacket on and I could swim. I had survived the sinking. I was fine. I was excited and there was no time to worry. Then fear kicked in as the falling bombs continued and the oil fuel from burst ships' tanks coated the water. After about twenty minutes in the water I was frozen and had to be lifted into the rescue boat that picked us up. I was transferred to *Schyt Hilda*, a Dutch coaster that had been requisitioned by the Navy and manned with a naval crew for the duration of the Dunkirk operation. Once on board *Hilda* oily clothes were peeled off and kind soldiers lent us great coats and we settled down in the warm sun for the journey home.

How slow it seemed to us. We never seemed to pass the town of Dunkirk, with its huge pall of black smoke rising hundreds of feet above it, and every minute was agony lest we be attacked again. At last we were out of the narrow sea lane running along that fatal strip of coast. At last we were heading for the open sea and for England. At last we could relax. One and all we fell asleep.

This was soon disturbed, however, by the old familiar cry 'Enemy aircraft', but this time they were our own, the first we had seen. A quarter of an hour later four more aircraft appeared and these were definitely unfriendly. Within the twinkling of an eye they had attacked and hit a nearby transport, then circled round like some fantastic birds of prey selecting their next victim. Would it be us? I held my breath, closed my eyes and waited.

Then we heard several explosions some way off and saw that two paddle steamers had been hit and were sinking. In a short time two destroyers and *Hilda* arrived on the scene to rescue the survivors. All the time the aircraft were still up top somewhere waiting to pounce. Swooping down they tried to bomb one of the destroyers but their missiles fell wide and they made off. Meanwhile, their two victims had sunk so rapidly that their boats had not been launched and the water was black with men who were quickly rescued. Once more we set off on our long and laborious way. The rest of the journey was made in peace though every yard was a suspense lest we should be robbed of the fruits of safety. Finally, about 6.30 pm, after the most eventful twenty-four hours of our lives, we reached Ramsgate, never more thankful to reach dry land.

This is the end of my story, written within a week of the loss of *Skipjack*. Nineteen of the Ship's Company were killed and a number wounded. Most of the 294 soldiers we had on board went down with the ship as they were all below decks. Afterwards I felt very sad that we had failed them. Once on board they had felt safe and on their way home and we had not managed to bring them home. Their number included a group of army parsons of all denominations whom we had put in the Captain's cabin. Earlier when I looked in on them while they were having coffee the naughty thought came into my mind that we might stand a better chance of survival as I assumed they had an emergency line to the Almighty and they would be praying like mad. Sadly their prayers were not answered. I was far too busy to pray. Despite the horror of it all I had absolutely no reaction, no nightmares, no flashbacks or psychosomatic illnesses. Today I would have been offered counselling and kept under close observation. All I wanted was a few days' rest and a good time and to get back to sea in another ship. The reason was we were young and fit and full of life.

It was only in 1985 that I got *Skipjack*'s casualty list from the Ministry of Defence. Until then I did not know which of my friends had been killed as we were dispersed to our homes after we landed at Ramsgate. Anyway, it was war and we did not mourn as we do now for our lost soldiers and sailors. When death is always close to you it's not something to dwell on and I quickly put Dunkirk behind me. Sixty-five years later I wrote a tribute to our nineteen dead and all the drowned soldiers in our local magazine for our Remembrance Day service in November 2005. I have included it as an appendix at the end of the book.

One last memory of that extraordinary June day in 1940 is our return to safety in England at Ramsgate. I landed stark naked in my birthday suit with a blanket draped round my shoulders. I was not the least embarrassed until a good lady in the Women's Voluntary Services offered me a cup of tea. How to drink a cup of tea standing up starko in a dockside shed? Lift cup to lips, blanket slides off. Tug it up and try again. Same result. Must sit down but where?

What a talent we have for reducing the dramas and horrors of life to the banal. Cups of tea and biscuits served by unflappable grannies is the national panacea and it works. The sheer ordinariness of watching scores of women bustling around dishing out cups of tea to all comers at all hours soothes the nerves and brings one back to normality. By the time I climbed into the coach, still clutching my faithful blanket, I had almost forgotten the morning's tragedy. All I craved was a decent pair of trousers to cover my nether parts and a shirt.

In the bus our crew survivors displayed that rather forced hilarity and intense cheerfulness that keeps disasters at bay.

At Chatham Naval Barracks the sheep were separated from the goats. 'Ratings fall in on the left: officers fall in on the right.'

This ensured we were issued with the distinctive clothing according to our rank. Protocol must always be preserved. As a Sub-Lieutenant I was dished out with a pyjama top as a shirt, a dilapidated sports jacket, a pair of trousers whose 'turn ups' came somewhere between my ankles and my knees, a pair of bedroom slippers and a sub for £5 and told to find my way home to Bexhill-on-Sea.

I caught the train to London Bridge and the tube to Victoria. I just had time to warn the family I was coming home on leave and hopped on to the Hastings train. Londoners did not appear to find my garb at all way out and by the time I reached Bexhill I had forgotten that I looked like a 'dosser'. Instead of the ecstatic welcome for the hero home from the sea my mother took one look at me.

'What are you doing in those dreadful clothes?' she asked.

Then I remembered I hadn't had time to tell her I was a survivor from Dunkirk and that many good friends had died that morning. As soon as I could I crawled into bed.

And that was the end of *Skipjack*, a modest little ship that had done nothing spectacular in the first year of the war. She had swept the vital convoy routes down the east coast from Tyneside to the Thames and all round the Scottish coast from Cape Wrath to the Moray Firth and made sure they were safe for shipping. She had rescued 865 soldiers from the Dunkirk beaches, where she now lay in twenty fathoms of water.

For me, it was the end of an era. A letter arrived confirming my automatic promotion to the rank of Lieutenant (two stripes). Goodbye *Skipjack*, what next?

In my anxiety to get back to sea I called in on the Admiralty to ask for a ship as soon as possible. A kindly Commander shooed me out of his office.

'Go home; have a good leave; we'll let you know in due course.'

He appeared to think I needed recuperation and rest. I didn't want more than a week's rest ashore and was concerned that I might miss the sea battle against the expected German invasion forces. By now the coasts of Europe from the North Cape in Norway to Normandy in France were under the enemy's control. Our army had lost most of its weapons; the RAF lost a number of aircraft in France and the Navy had suffered severe destroyer and minesweeper losses off the Belgian and French coasts. Britain was wide open to airborne and seaborne attack.

Chapter Six

Boredom and Excitements

Minesweeping 1939–1942

Afffter Dunkirk the country knew we had our backs to the wall. France had surrendered and we were on our own. This was the time that Churchill fired up the people of Britain with his rousing speeches.

'We will fight on the beaches; we will fight in the streets; we will fight in the hills … we will never surrender.'

He brought the whole country to the boil. Never was there such unanimity of purpose. Class divisions were swept aside and everyone prepared to repel the invader. Dads' Armies were formed though they had no weapons and young boys as young as fourteen played their part as messengers. Old ladies made poisoned cakes to offer to the invading German paratroopers. All signposts were removed and anyone asking their way and looking the least suspicious was assumed to be a Nazi paratrooper. Nuns had a bad time as scare stories had been spread that one elite German airborne regiment had been dropped in Holland dressed as nuns with machine-guns hidden under their habits.

All boys and girls aged eighteen were conscripted for the Services and, unlike in World War I, they all had to start at the bottom and go through the ranks. Old Etonians and boys from the Glasgow Gorbals shared the same experience. My brother who later became headmaster of Eton told me he learned more about life from his fifteen months on the lower deck of the Royal Navy than any other experience in his life.

We all felt totally committed to defeating the expected invasion. The Navy was still much stronger than the German Navy and, I believe, would have wrecked their seaborne invasion, but would the army have been able to contain their airborne forces as they had lost almost all their weapons? The key was the RAF, which was undefeated. It would have been a close run thing.

I was obsessed with getting back to sea before the invasion started. I wanted to be part of the battle in the Channel, which would decide the fate of the country. It was the only time during the war that I really felt ready and willing to die for my country.

After what seemed an age an Admiralty letter dropped on the doormat.

'You are appointed First Lieutenant of HMS *Bridlington*. You are to report to Messrs William Denny's Shipyard at Dumbarton, where *Bridlington* is completing construction, on 22nd June 1940.' *Bridlington* was another fleet minesweeper like *Skipjack*, but bang up to date. This was just what I wanted, a step up the ladder, since the First Lieutenant was also second in command and took over if the Captain was killed or disabled. This could lead to a command in a year's time.

When a ship is under construction a few key people are attached to the shipyard to oversee the final preparations for taking the ship to sea. Our team consisted of the Engineer Officer, three skilled engine room artificers and I. The engineers checked every piece of machinery as it was installed, main engines, fire pumps, winches and derricks. I was consulted on the exact positioning of seamanship and navigating gear and weapons equipment. It wasn't exacting work. The ship's hull was in dry dock and most of the deck equipment was still to be fitted. I looked at her on that first day and wondered what her fate would be. Would she survive all hazards or would she, like *Skipjack*, eventually sit on the bottom of the North Sea a coffin to some of her crew. Too much imagination. I did not dwell on it. Now we had to get her ready for the tasks that lay ahead.

The Battle of Britain was about to be unleashed over southern England and the sooner we could get to sea the better. We might be needed for the anti-invasion defence in the Dover straits.

Denny's Shipyard on the Clyde west of Glasgow was still a family-run business and extremely friendly. After a not particularly strenuous forenoon on board the ship's officers joined the family and senior managers for lunch in the boardroom. Then a final totter round the ship after lunch to review progress and off to my digs at 4 pm.

There was no naval presence at Dumbarton and when I arrived I was given the address of a landlady who would provide lodgings until we sailed in September. Mrs Hudson was a lovely middle-aged Scottish lady whose husband worked as a foreman in John Brown's shipyard further up the Clyde.

After a long journey from the south coast to Glasgow I arrived in time for 'tea'. Tea in middle class homes at that time consisted of a genteel 'cuppa', delicately cut sandwiches and some cakes. This tea was of an entirely more robust character. It was the main cooked evening meal for the workers of the family returning from a heavy day's work. Every evening, about 5 pm, I joined the family for this meal and soon felt as if I was one of them. They looked after me as if I was one of their own.

On this my first day I thought I should leave the family after the meal and retired to my room to unpack and sort out the pile of 'bumph' I had been issued with to guide me through the next few weeks. That night I was just getting into my pyjamas at 10 pm, weary after a long day's travel, when there was a knock on my door.

My landlady called out 'Will ye no come down for a cup of tea?'

A cup of tea was the last thing I wanted but I felt it was important not to be standoffish so I quickly dressed and joined the family for a 'cuppa'. On the table was spread every conceivable sort of home-baked scones, baps, as well as honey, jam and lashings of tea. This was a feeding routine I soon got used to.

When the men of the family got to know me better and discovered that I wasn't the posh twit that my cut glass accent suggested they sometimes gathered me up after tea and took me to the nearest pub. Now I was well accustomed to several tots of an evening when *Skipjack* was in harbour but nothing could have prepared me for Scottish boozing. The aim of many was to become utterly legless, stoned out of their minds, before the pub closed at 10.30 pm.

There was a lethal custom of buying 'rounds' of drinks where everyone in the group, in turn, bought everyone else in the group a drink. A 'round' consisted of a tot of whiskey, always a double in Scotland, followed immediately by a pint of beer. Serious stuff – binge drinking 1940 style.

Although I enjoyed a few drinks on a 'run ashore' I hated the idea of losing control of myself and had, up to that point, always succeeded in remaining upright and reasonably conscious. I was determined not to succumb now. I found that if I paid for one of the first two rounds the company had a tendency to overlook me as the evening wore on. Occasionally, if pressed to another unwanted drink it would simply provide refreshment to an aspidistra. Anyway, I remained upright and so did the other members of the family because they had to face 'mother' when we got home and that spread of food.

These weeks with Mrs Hudson and her family was an education for me and I was most grateful to them for accepting me in their midst. While I enjoyed these weeks ashore I felt I ought to be at sea, not living the life of Riley in safety and comfort.

At weekends when I felt I needed time for reflection I would walk out of Dumbarton and climb in the Kilpatrick Hills where I could gaze down on the beautiful Firth of Clyde and feel mentally refreshed. Like a speck in the distance amongst the gantries and cranes of the shipyard lay my new ship and I pondered what the future might bring. In the solitude of the hills the war seemed a long way off. This undemanding existence was an astonishing contrast to life at sea, minesweeping. I wondered if I was getting soft. One evening as I scampered down the hillside I stumbled on a couple actively copulating. Life must go on.

August came and I was allowed two weeks' summer leave, unheard of since the start of the war. I went home to Belstone in Devon in the far south-west, to Dartmoor and a life untouched by the war. My mother had been thrown out of her home at Bexhill at short notice as it was needed to be turned into a fortification as part of the sea defences against the invasion.

Luckily she was able to rent a cottage at Belstone where we had spent several holidays and she stayed there for the rest of the war. Most of the young farm workers were in reserved occupations and had not been called up for military service and village life had not changed, though it did later. It was a wonderful experience for a short time but it made me uneasy as the onslaught by the *Luftwaffe* was hotting up and invasion seemed near. Would *Bridlington* be ready in time?

The nucleus crew was issued with pistols with which to defend the shipyard in case of attack by paratroopers and every time the air raid sirens wailed we met in the High Street and marched down to the yard. There was virtually no danger as we were about as far away from the action as it was possible to be. Nevertheless, we took our duties seriously and I even became an adviser to the Waterborne Home Guard (Dad's Army) on Loch Lomond. Despite my doubts the Guard Commander was convinced that we would face a waterborne landing by seaplanes on the loch. After discussing waterborne tactics in such an unlikely event it gave me a pleasant evening on the loch and a few drams afterwards in a lovely pub by the water's edge.

September came and the Battle of Britain was raging. Huge battalions of German bombers were assaulting the airfields of southern England to defeat the RAF before launching their invasion. Despite being outnumbered our Hurricanes and Spitfires succeeded in shooting down many of the enemy but the balance of victory was still undecided. It was believed that the date for the German D-Day was 21 September with seaborne landings between Brighton and Portsmouth and parachute landings inland to secure the South Downs.

On 21 September we heard the church bells ringing and this was the signal for an imminent invasion. The bells had been silenced since the start of the war and they were reserved for this special warning. Had the invasion started we all wondered. Although the RAF had incurred heavy losses the *Luftwaffe* had not succeeded in destroying their fighting capacity.

Far away in the north I worried about my mother in the south and my two young brothers also at school in the south. The alarm did not last long and the bells fell silent again and I don't think they were rung again until victory, VE Day, in May 1945.

Many of us thought this alarm was a precaution by the government to keep everyone on their toes. The failure of the *Luftwaffe* to defeat the RAF and their inability to close the Dover Straits to our convoys made them change their minds and make two fatal mistakes. They diverted their air attacks on to the softer target of London and they attacked Russia in the spring of 1941.

In the last two weeks of September the RAF shot down large numbers of enemy aircraft and 21 September was probably the turning point in the Battle of Britain.

Now our ship was nearly ready. The finishing touches were applied: coats of paint; carpets to be chosen; curtains for the messdecks; anchors and cables to be stowed. Soon we would be off at last. I was impatient to get out to the oceans to test our minesweeping gear and ourselves.

The greatest day for a new ship had arrived, her commissioning as one of His Majesty's Ships. A completely new crew arrived by overnight train from Portsmouth. Meanwhile, an army of cleaners, charwomen they were called in those days, scrubbed the living quarters from top to bottom. I had never seen such a clean ship. The yard had done a fantastic job and the ship literally glistened from bow to stern.

I met the crew on arrival just before noon and escorted them to a local restaurant where we had laid on a hot lunch. The usual naval 'bag' meal didn't seem appropriate after such a long journey and the Captain and I had decided to do them proud on their first day. We were not sure whether the authorities would pay but that could wait.

As I walked round the tables to chat to them I sensed they were a good lot. Despite their long journey they were cheerful and full of lower deck repartee. I was sizing them up and they were sizing me up.

Most of them looked like children, conscripts of eighteen to nineteen years of age, peppered by a few older RN regulars. Many of them had never been to sea. I felt very old and experienced after four and a half years at sea. Then it hit me I was only twenty-one, hardly a veteran.

We had much work to do before dark. All the provisions and stores lay on the dockside and had to be humped on board and stowed in their proper positions. Coached to the shipyard the new boys set to with great gusto and the job was done before suppertime, which the cooks had managed to produce on the newly lit stoves. Our Captain was delighted with the crew and the way they worked. When I did my night rounds there were questions as to the future, which I answered as best I could. (Each night before lights out an officer walks round the messdecks to see that they have been cleared up and everything is shipshape.)

The next day the Captain told the Ship's Company what our programme was. The Captain was a tall, blond, handsome Viking, only four years older than me and he had done my present job for the previous eighteen months and was an expert minesweeper. Like me he was Dartmouth trained and as regular as they come. Our Engineer Officer was a Royal Naval Reserve Merchant Navy Officer who was a wizard engineer, particularly knowledgeable on diesel engines, which was useful as we were one of the first RN ships to be fitted with diesels. His other claim to fame was that whenever we went into port there was always a woman waiting for him, a 'wife' in every port. He was unmarried, fat, bald and forty-five and had an extraordinary fascination for the ladies. There were only two other officers, a young navigator, Sub-Lieutenant RN, doing the same job that I had done in *Skipjack*, a shy, likeable twenty-year-old. The last member of the wardroom was a thirty-year-old Royal Naval Volunteer Reserve Officer, an insurance executive in peacetime who proved a most diligent and effective watchkeeping officer. We had to live with each other in the coming months and avoid getting on each other's nerves. In a small ship if the wardroom officers fall out it is disastrous. As usual in the Navy the Captain kept much to himself but joined us for meals in the wardroom.

We had to 'shake down' quickly and get to know each other's strengths and weaknesses as we were almost immediately off to sea down the Clyde for our sea trials. At this stage the ship had not entered naval service and was a shared responsibility with the shipyard. Before *Bridlington* could belong to His Majesty every item of equipment had to be tested. We fired all the guns, dropped depth charges, did speed trials to check out the engines and practised firefighting and damage repair. Every piece of equipment had to be rigorously tested to its limits.

When all this had been accomplished the Admiral responsible for accepting ships from civilian shipyards came on board with his staff and inspected the ship from top to bottom. When he finished and was satisfied he and the Captain were expected to sign the acceptance document, taking *Bridlington* into naval service.

For some weeks our young Captain had been complaining to the shipyard that the engine noise from the main diesel engines exhausting through the funnel was deafening and the bridge crew would never be able to hear approaching aircraft. He and I had both had experience of dive-bomber attacks where, in those days before radar, we relied on hearing to alert the guns crews. We wanted silencers fitted in the funnel but the shipyard kept saying 'Not in the specification'. After the Admiral had signed the acceptance document the Captain was expected to sign and he, courageously, said 'I'm not signing'. Uproar. No one refused to sign such a document; it was merely a formality. Ticky Malins pointed to the wording. 'HMS *Bridlington* is, in all respects ready for war and fit to go to sea'.

'She's not,' he said. 'I'm not signing until the silencers are fitted.' And a few days later they were and we were seaworthy and battleworthy.

Steaming down the Clyde must be one of the most beautiful sea passages in the UK. As you turn to port past Gourock the Isle of Arran lifts itself out of the sea into the clouds and the lush green fields of Ayrshire pass down the port side. Ahead lies the Irish Sea, the open sea where the war lies in wait.

Suddenly, as I saw the Channel opening and the ocean's distant horizon I was assailed by a spasm of fear, so unexpected that it threw me for a moment. I didn't want to go out to the war again. Apprehension as to the future hit me. 'Go back to the soft days ashore where you were not required to steel yourself to face the unseen enemy' a little devil whispered to me. This weakness was quickly banished but for a few minutes it had clutched my innards and I was ashamed. I was also surprised as, from the minute I had stepped ashore at Ramsgate in June, I had longed to get back to sea again and into the fray. This enthusiasm had faded in the weeks ashore.

In peace and war I had always enjoyed being at sea, such a capricious mistress. One moment sparkling and dancing under a blue summer sky: the next fierce and storm-driven with cruel waves hovering over you and breaking in a cascade like falling snow. Always changing, always beautiful. That sea and hard work soon restored me as we learned to do our job, sweep mines.

We steamed north past the Western Isles with the towering peaks of the Cuillins to starboard and felt the deep ocean swell as we left the shelter of the mainland. To starboard round Cape Wrath and along that castellated north coast, which rises sheer out of the sea all the way to Duncansby Head and John O'Groats, where I had spent many long days sweeping mines in *Skipjack* the previous winter. Past the Old Man of Hoy, a perpendicular rock splinter sticking out of the sea at the entrance to our anchorage in the Sound of Hoy, that miserable corner of Scapa Flow, as bleak and inhospitable part of the world as can be imagined. We now faced many more winter months there but I preferred being at sea.

Although I had spent over a year minesweeping I had never been in charge of the sweep deck right aft. None of our crew had seen a sweep wire. So we were all novices together and if you get your sweep wires crossed on the sweep deck you are in serious trouble.

The vital part of the minesweeping gear were the two sweep wires, designed to cut the mooring wire that tied the mine to its sinker weight, which lay on the seabed. These wires were wound round two large drums on the quarterdeck and both of these had to be let out (streamed) to their full extent. The far end of each wire was attached to a kite, only this was an underwater kite not a sky kite. This looked just like a sky kite but was made of steel and was designed to keep the sweep wire under the water. To mark the end of the sweep wire there was a float, which looked like a dolphin and if you weren't careful it behaved like one, diving under the sea and shooting up into the sky, causing all sorts of problems. This dolphin was connected to the kite at the end of the sweep wire and controlled the depth of the sweep. The longer the wire the deeper the sweep. Thus there was a lot of 'knitting' lying around on the sweep deck before the order 'Out sweeps' was ordered from the bridge. The best sweep decks were controlled in silence, using hand signals to the Chief Petty Officer Stoker, a key man controlling the speed of laying out the two wires from the winches, and a quiet voice up the intercom to the Captain.

My job was to stand right aft looking over the ship's stern to make sure the wires were streaming at the correct angle, about forty-five degrees. If the wires sagged to the vertical there was a danger they might drag along the bottom and snag on a rock or wreck and there was a danger a wire could part causing casualties on the sweep deck. There was a symphony to be played between the ship's speed and the speed of streaming the wires. They had to be in tune and the Captain on the bridge and I had to work closely together. All this I still had to learn.

We had two weeks to perfect our minesweeping skills before being let loose on the convoy routes. None of my sweep deck crew had seen a sweep wire before and I had to explain every little detail to them, but as I had not actually been on the sweep deck in *Skipjack* it was rather a case of the partially blind leading the blind. We learned the hard way by making elementary mistakes, greatly assisted by our Captain's words of encouragement from the bridge.

'You stupid … pull your f… fingers out. Get the float out first, slowly with the wire or the sweep will part.'

'Come and do it yourself,' I muttered under my breath.

We soon got the hang of it and became a slick and efficient minesweeping crew. The Captain even said 'Well done' one day. Under training we were sweeping sand-filled mines but now we were ready for the real thing.

The correct streaming of sweeps was just a matter of coordinated timing of each sequence and after a month we could do it blindfold. On the other hand the recovery of sweeps was more hazardous.

At set lengths along the sweep wires cutters like giant scissors were fitted to cut the mooring wires of the mines. Sometimes these cutters failed to cut the mine wire and the mine would get stuck in the cutter, waiting to explode when it hit the ship's stern as the sweep wire was wound in. All the time the sweep wires were being wound in I would stand as far aft as I could and lean over the stern, watching the sweep wires like an eagle looking for its prey. There was usually some indication of the peril of a mine in the sweep because the mine dragged the sweep wire and altered its angle of recovery, but not always. The worst scenario was when a mine was stuck in the far end of the sweep, which made it difficult to detect. As the last few feet of wire are wound in the kite and the wire end drop almost vertically under the ship's stern. I would be peering into the dark green sea watching for this black cylinder with its sinister fingers pointing up at me, the detonators. 'Mine in the sweep' I would call to the Captain. To the Chief Stoker I would give an urgent rotary hand signal in an anti-clockwise direction to tell him to reverse the direction of the sweep wire drums and gently let the wires unwind to give more distance from the ship. 'Clear the sweep deck' I would say to the rest of the crew. If the ship's stern is blown off they might be spared whereas I would be in small pieces and suffering no pain.

Slowly the black football disappears astern as the Captain increases the ship's speed and the wire unwinds. A moment of excitement and all over in less than a minute. It happened seldom but every time we recovered sweeps I had to be extremely vigilant as those last few feet of wire came inboard.

Getting sweeps in and out was satisfying and once the crew was trained we all appreciated each other's role and it worked like clockwork. It brought officers and men much closer together than in the big ships. In a small minesweeper officers and men all hauled on the same rope. Protocol didn't bother us much and the sweep deck crew looked like a bunch of pirates in their overalls, wellies and balaclavas. My sweep deck uniform consisted of blue corduroy trousers, no cap and a uniform jacket so that if I was captured the Germans would know I was an officer. The work was too dirty for smart clothes.

Whenever the sweeps were streamed I had to remain close to the quarterdeck ready for any emergency. Every day, as we had done in *Skipjack*, we went to sea at the first glimmer of daylight and steamed out to our sweeping station in the Pentland Firth to make sure the convoy route round the north of Scotland was safe. Because the Channel route was so dangerous now that the enemy was ensconced in airfields in France most ships bound for London and the east coast ports were routed round the northern coasts. Sometimes for a change we swept the Home Fleet out of Scapa Flow into the North Sea. It was cold and dull with very few mines. It was equally dull in harbour where there was no civilisation and nothing to do ashore. When we got into harbour in the evenings there was nothing but work and drink to alleviate the boredom. Some officers drank too much. Gin was two old pennies a tot and naval gin was far more powerful than the shore stuff. Only occasionally were we reminded that there was a war on.

It was about this time that I had an unnerving experience every night. It lasted for four days and then stopped as suddenly as it had begun. As I lay in my bunk trying to get to sleep I distinctly heard the noise of a torpedo coming towards the ship's side exactly where I was lying. The noise started some way off, quite faintly, and then it got louder and louder as it drew near the ship. Just as it was about to explode it stopped. Silence. I realised it was a phantom but it scared me. I could think of no reason why I should be imagining this as I was no more stressed than usual. Possibly a late flashback from my swim at Dunkirk? Anyway, it never recurred.

So far the newly fledged *Bridlington* had had no baptism of fire. Then one day in the Moray Firth she had her first encounter with an enemy aircraft. A single plane high in a cloud strewn sky. We pooped off our big guns but got nowhere near it. My action station was to control the 4-inch gun on the foc'sle. The enemy disappeared into the clouds and I tried to find it with my binoculars (still no radar). Standing on the open deck, gazing at the sky, I did not at first notice a pretty line of bright sparks running across the deck towards to me then I wondered what it was as it passed by me. One of the gun's crew spotted the aircraft, which was firing at us with his machine-gun. 'Sir, he's machine-gunning us,' he shouted. The line of the sparks was where the bullets were hitting the steel deck. I suffered no ill effects and my standing with the gun's crew went sky high as they thought I was showing amazing sangfroid (or sheer stupidity). Actually, I hadn't a clue what the sparks were and thought they might have been caused by someone welding in the cable locker below. As soon as I heard the warning I dived for cover mighty quickly. It was a 0–0 result as the enemy disappeared back home and we went on with our sweeping undamaged.

Not long afterwards a more serious incident hit us. By wartime standards it was a very minor disaster, one amongst many far worse tragedies. But this one has haunted my memory more than most. The 9th minesweeping flotilla was returning to Invergordon after a long day's sweep in the Moray Firth. I was on watch on the bridge. A lone German bomber swooped out of low storm clouds and landed a bomb on the bows of HMS *Bangor*, our flotilla leader. The whole of her fore deck peeled back as far as the bridge, like a tin of sardines being opened. A disembodied voice came up the voicepipe from the wireless office.

'Bridge this is wireless office. Gale Warning. South westerly gale force 8–9 expected shortly.'

It was getting darker already. The wind was howling in the rigging and the sea was whipping up into white foam with deep troughs between the waves. The only hope for *Bangor* was to be towed backwards to Invergordon, but getting towing wires across in this weather would be a miracle. After many attempts HMS *Rhyl* succeeded in passing a towing wire over to her but it soon parted as the ships rose and fell in the mounting swell. *Bangor* was wallowing out of control in the heavy seas.

Her Captain ordered *Rhyl* to steam up alongside to take off as many men as possible. The two ships were dropping and rising more than twenty feet in the stormy sea and timing a jump from one ship to the other with the waves sweeping down the decks needed split second judgment. A false leap and you were squashed like the jam in a sandwich between the two ships.

By now a full gale was blowing and a dense black night had descended. All ships played their searchlights round the stricken ship and the effect on the sea and sky was to light up an inferno of crashing waves and lowering clouds, which was absolutely terrifying. We felt a crippling helplessness. *Rhyl* could not stay alongside and *Bangor*'s bows were digging deeper into the inky sea as the forepart of the ship filled with water. She was near her end.

'Bridge this is wireless office. Signal from *Bangor*. Am abandoning ship.'

That last heartrending cry from doomed ships. There was little hope of picking up any survivors out of the sea in such a gale. Ships threw their life rafts into the sea in the vain hope that some might be able to scramble into them. We saw none. Soon her bows angled down into the waves and she slid gracefully under the raging sea. Her propellers were still turning as she sank.

With heavy hearts we returned to Invergordon. There is nothing worse than watching a ship sink at sea when you can do so little to help.

With a bang we had been reminded of the perils that might suddenly be unleashed on us. The next day we were sweeping in the same area and too engrossed in our work to grieve much for the loss of friends, including one of my Drake term mates. Why didn't we grieve more? These occasions, like the loss of *Skipjack* at Dunkirk, are too close to home. We didn't want to be reminded of the fragility of our existence. So, 'Bad luck mates I'm all right but it may be my turn tomorrow and I would rather not think about it'. Such was war; move on; don't dwell on sadness. It sounds heartless now but it was a shield against fear.

Soon after these diversions we were ordered to leave Scapa. We all gave three cheers; it had been a bleak and stormy winter where the real enemy was the weather and the sea. We were to anchor in the Kyle of Lochalsh, a beautiful loch between the Isle of Skye and the mainland. It was the loveliest place to be based and as peaceful as my Dartmoor with the mighty Cuillins to the west and the Scottish Highlands on the mainland, a feast of beauty. The war seemed remote.

Our new job was the same as I had done before the war in the Dover Straits, skimming the tops of our own minefields to ensure they were safe for our own ships to pass over the top of them without blowing up. This minefield was being laid between the Orkney Islands and Iceland in what was called the Iceland Gap, which was the area where the submerged U-boats sailed into the Atlantic. The minefield was designed to catch them as they passed through the Gap.

The late winter weather in the far north was even bleaker than in the Pentland Firth. Our forward sweeping base was in the Faroe Islands, as barren and unforgiving a spot as I have ever enjoyed. Even worse than Scapa. The inhabitants were tough fishermen and nominally the islands belonged to Denmark, but I don't think they paid much attention to Copenhagen.

The minesweeping drill was the same as usual: out into the northern darkness to where the minelayers were operating; 'out sweeps'; form up in our sweeping positions and plough up and down the lines of mines. Soon the sirens were tootling to warn that a mine had been cut and had surfaced. There it was ahead of us; a large black blob bumping along in the waves. Each ship's sharpshooters had a go at blowing it up as it passed down the formation. The shooting was rather more hazardous than the mine. In this particular minefield there was much faulty depth keeping and we had to be on our toes to spot the rogues as they bubbled to the surface.

Minelaying requires reasonably calm weather so when the long-range forecast was dire we retired to the Kyle of Lochalsh for maintenance and recreation. For recreation some of us would land on Skye and walk in the foothills. We couldn't try any serious climbing as we had to be able to get quickly back on board in case we were ordered to sea. We had some fantastic walks on frozen grass with the snow-covered Cuillins looking so tantalising close. In the evening short leave from 16.30 hours to midnight was given to the Ship's Company but the delights of Lochalsh were limited and most of the men preferred to stay on board. In those days, before mobile phones and television, the ship was isolated except for the radio. Uckers (naval ludo) was a staple game as well as all sorts of card games from bridge to rummy and whist. Gambling was not allowed but almost certainly occurred. We entertained ourselves and provided the mail arrived on time we were reasonably content.

The only entertainment ashore was at one small hotel, the Kyle Hotel, the top half of which had been taken over as the offices of the Naval Officer in Charge, Lochalsh, but sensibly the Navy had not requisitioned the ground floor where there was a dining room and a lovely bar looking out over the loch to Skye beyond. After a pleasant evening wining and dining I can recall a moonlight night when we chuntered slowly back to the ship in our little motor boat, surrounded by the breathtaking beauty of the full moon shining on the great white hills of the Highlands, singing the old songs as we puttered along over a silvery sea. We always gave a finale with the Song of the Minesweepers, sung to the tune of Hymn 95

> Holy, Holy, Holy, Lord God Almighty,
> Early in the morning our song shall rise to thee.
> Holy, Holy, Holy, merciful and mighty
> God in three persons Blessed Trinity.

Our somewhat different version was:

> Sweeping, Sweeping, Sweeping, always fucking well sweeping,
> Early in the morning we rise and sweep the seas,
> Sweeping, sweeping, sweeping, always fucking well sweeping.
> In storm and sunshine always out at sea.

What extraordinary contrasts war throws up. Perhaps it was one of the ways we were able to cope with it for years on end.

I didn't know at the time but a few months earlier my future wife, Angela, had started her naval career as a lowly messenger in the signal offices in the naval headquarters. Years later we both retraced our steps and stayed in the hotel.

These idyllic intervals never lasted long and we were soon back to the icy, stormy waters of the Iceland Gap. After two more weeks our task was nearly done and we wondered 'What next?'

Much to our surprise we were ordered to steam south, as far south as we could possibility go, to the Channel. Initially the news hit me hard. Sweeping mines in those waters with our sweeps streamed astern of us and unable to manoeuvre we would be easy targets for dive-bombers. We would be within twenty minutes' flying time of numerous German air bases along the French coast and I imagined Dunkirk all over again. I needed to keep my feelings tightly buttoned up. The men were thrilled to be nearer most of their homes in the southern counties.

The start of the journey south was spectacular, through the narrow passage of Kyle Rhea, now an otter sanctuary, and on down the Sound of Sleat, past the islands of Eigg, Muck and Rum and briefly out into the Atlantic swell. Farewell to the mountains and hills of the Highlands, which had softened the cares of war and reminded us of another world, unchanging and unaffected by man's little troubles. On down the Irish Sea and ahead of us the Cornish cliffs loomed up and the light of the Wolf Rock lighthouse, guarding the Isles of Scilly, threw its warning beams towards us and made sure our navigation was correct. At daybreak we rounded Land's End and steamed up the south Cornish coast to Falmouth.

Our new task was to keep the south coast convoy route clear of mines. The large ships of the Atlantic convoys were still going north about but the Channel was being increasingly used for coastal shipping. Our stretch ran from Falmouth to the Isle of Wight and our sweeping practice was very different to our northern experiences. The harbours were close to the convoy routes and we quickly reached our sweep start each morning and swept along the coast until sunset. Night sweeping was not possible in those days and as each day closed we bustled into the nearest port for the night and, if there was time, a quick run ashore. We got to know Fowey, Dartmouth, Poole and Yarmouth in the Isle of Wight, delightful little harbours that somehow fitted our little ships and were all close to our minesweeping areas. The Ship's Company enjoyed the numerous pubs when we tied up alongside in Poole, sometimes with dire results.

I was not taken completely by surprise one night in Fowey when the Duty Petty Officer woke me at 1 am.

'Duty Petty Officer, sir'

'What is it?' I replied rather grumpily as I had only just got to sleep.

'It's Rutherford, sir'.

Now Rutherford was one of our crosses. He was a first class seaman and I liked his blunt Glaswegian manner – when he was sober. But when he went for a 'run ashore' he acted as if he was in Glasgow and imbibed accordingly. He invented binge drinking.

'He's got a knife, sir'.

In those days Glaswegians liked to 'cut up' those they took a dislike to and a knife was part of their kit, but not on board His Majesty's Ships. I sensed there was some sort of crisis. We went down to the messdeck and found an extremely inebriated Rutherford waving a knife around and threatening all and sundry. He was so drunk the knife was unlikely to hit any target. As soon as he saw me a stream of totally incomprehensible Glaswegian poured forth and it was clear he had some sort of grievance against the world in general and his messmates in particular.

Rather inadequately I asked him, 'What's the trouble, Rutherford?'

This prompted a further flood of invective. My Dartmouth training had not included coping with an armed sailor bent on sorting out his messmates but I had always had a good relationship with Rutherford so I tried again.

'Tell me what's the matter Rutherford.'

This launched him on another tirade but he began to calm down and gradually ran out of steam.

'I think you had better give me your knife and I will keep it for you,' I said hopefully. This was a bit of a gamble but it worked and as he handed over the weapon he subsided on to the deck in his drunken stupor. A guard was placed over him for the night, mainly for his own safety, as drunkards can drown in their vomit and may need rapid first aid. It never happened again.

My premonition of fighting off hordes of dive-bombers was proved to be totally unsubstantiated. We were never attacked at sea, although occasionally in harbour. Despite the lack of enemy air attacks Their Lordships of the Admiralty decided we needed more protection from the *Stukas* and sent each ship a personal barrage balloon.

From the outbreak of the war the big cities had been protected by these huge sausages floating above them to deter low-level bombing. Now it was the turn of the ships. The Channel-bound merchant ships had been supplied with these marine balloons and they had been effective in fending off the dive-bombers. The crew was greatly chuffed when we were selected to become a balloon-equipped ship, but it was disappointing when the balloon arrived that it fitted into a suitcase. Soon we were off to sea on our first great balloon day – B day.

As First Lieutenant I was responsible to the Captain for all upper deck activities. Naturally the balloon would come under my orders. Who should be the Balloon Officer? Me of course.

We cleared the harbour entrance and pumped up the balloon in the shelter of the bridge and it looked quite impressive when fully inflated. It then had to be taken right up to the bows of the ship to be tethered to the balloon's sky wire, which was on a reel waiting to be unwound so that the great sausage could soar up into the sky above us and deter the dive-bombers. As this was our first shot at raising the balloon I decided that such an important occasion required my personal attention. On future occasions a trained balloon rating (Able Seaman) would take over.

I held the inflated balloon on a short 'tail' wire to take it up to the bows to be shackled to its sky wire. As I advanced up the foc'sle a strong gust of wind caught the balloon and in a trice it was taking off with me on the end. I struggled to control it but it had a will of its own and soon I was soaring up into the sky (or so I thought). In fact, I was only about six feet off the deck.

No one was coming to my assistance. They were all paralysed with laughter. I realised that if I hung on much longer I would be amongst the birds so I let go and landed in a heap on the deck. The balloon soared away into the stratosphere. Would I have to pay for it? Had I wilfully lost an important item of Admiralty stores, one Mark 2 balloon and associated sky wire? What a crime. My Captain was rude to me but no further action was taken. Soon afterwards all these balloons were withdrawn from the minesweepers as being impracticable. It was one of my life's special moments, which I treasure.

By this stage of the war, summer 1941, minesweeping was much less intense and finding a mine was a rarity, but we continued ensuring that the southern convoy lanes were safe. When the occasional mine floated to the surface and the sharpshooters spiked the detonators there was an almighty bang and, if it was safe to stop, a splendid catch of fish. Free of air attacks and a scarcity of mines made summer sweeping in the Channel rather enjoyable. The sea glittered in the sunlight; an empty sky spreading out to the far distant horizon and the flotilla steaming quietly along, their 'tails' trawling the ocean depths. A strangely peaceful scene and a pleasing sense of achievement.

The only darkness in this happy scene was the news of the war going on beyond us. While our little war had become rather cosy the war in the big world outside was not going our way. The Russians were in full retreat before a triumphant German army and our army in North Africa was seesawing back and forth between Benghazi in Libya and El Alamein in Egypt. British cities were suffering heavy casualties in night raids and some of the Ship's Company had wives and children caught up in them. When we heard on the early morning news that Portsmouth or Birmingham had been bombed there would be worried faces on deck. Then the misery of waiting to hear from loved ones, or much worse, the dreaded signal.

'Regret to inform you that Mary Smith, wife of Able Seaman John Smith, was killed during the raid on Birmingham on the night of 3rd June.' It only happened once to our crew. The stricken man was immediately landed to sort out his family and arrange the funeral. If he could not make satisfactory arrangements for the care of any children he would be given long leave. Otherwise he would return to the ship and get on with it. Possibly this was the right answer to grief; being busy and in company with good friends helped him through his misery. I felt it was sadder when a wife or child was killed than a fighting man. In World War II many civilians died and this was the big difference between that war and World War I.

For routine maintenance, a sort of MOT for our diesel engines, we occasionally went alongside the jetty in Poole in Dorset for three days. Nearby was Bournemouth, that watering hole of the wealthy. We were at sea most of the time and then life was intense and teetotal. So when we could get ashore we were inclined to let our hair right down. One evening after a tot or two in the wardroom several of us decided to cheer up Bournemouth. In those days Bournemouth was like an elderly dowager, prim and proper and deadly dull. When we got off the bus we found ourselves on the steps of the Grand Hotel, one of those vast mausoleums looking like St Pancras Station.

During the war the elderly rich could avoid food rationing and other wartime inconveniences by staying in such places and I have to admit many in the fighting services nursed a slight grudge against those who escaped the rigours of war in this way. This was unfair, particularly when many south coast towns were later bombed, but youth has always been critical.

Be that as it may we decided to cheer up the 'old dears' in the Grand. How bored they must be sitting amongst the potted palms listening to an ageing pianist tinkling away in the corner. Surely they would enjoy a jolly good sing song of naval shanties, nothing vulgar. Being in uniform we were conspicuous and we ordered a round of extremely expensive drinks. Perhaps we were a trifle noisy because one or two old gents rustled their newspapers and looked at us as if to see which hole we had crawled out of. Undaunted we gave them a rousing chorus of 'What shall we do with the drunken sailor'. No appreciation whatsoever. Deathly hush. Some of the dowagers tottered to the stairs.

Then a posse of polished managers descended on us like red-necked turkey cocks.

'Out out,' they cried. 'We shall call the police.'.

'Disgraceful,' twittered the 'old dears'.

We roared with laughter, but, being officers and gentlemen, we offered no resistance and allowed ourselves to be ejected. In today's world would we be called yobs? I am always careful when I come across youthful high spirits before condemning them. It may just be they are letting off steam and if you can't be high spirited when you are young when can you be?

Throughout the summer this comparatively peaceful life continued, leaving harbour at dawn. 'Out sweeps' on arrival at the convoy route. Then up and down the Channel – Portland Bill, Berry Head, near Torquay and then into Dartmouth for the night. Next day, on past Start Point, Rame Head in Cornwall and into the lovely little haven at Fowey. The next day we returned the same way. Each day the same – it was almost boring. So a little excitement was welcome. We received a signal from our flotilla leader: '*Bridlington* proceed independently towards Ventnor (in the Isle of Wight). Unidentified object has been reported in Sandown Bay, possibly a new type of mine. Recover and tow to Portsmouth.'

It was always important to recover new weapons as soon as possible so that the scientists could get to work on the countermeasures.

Off we went on our own and eventually spotted a black torpedo–like tube floating nose upright and dipping up and down in the sea and we could not recognise it as one of our old friends. We decided to treat it as a new device and with great caution. The Captain decided I should take personal charge of the recovery effort. We decided to use the whaler, which was propelled by oars, as the motor boat's engines might set it off if it was an acoustic device. We rowed gently up to it and circled round it so that I could inspect it at close quarters. I knew most of the enemy mines by sight, but this was a new one to me. Fortunately it had an eyebolt, a small steel ring, on its nose from which we could tow it. I made the crew cluster in the back of the boat, not that it would have made any difference if it had blown up, and tied the tow rope to the ring. We backed away from the mine and slowly let out the tow rope to a safe length and rowed back to the ship where the tow was transferred to the sweep deck. Once the tow was secured the Captain slowly moved the ship ahead and we headed for Portsmouth. On the way we were met by a dockyard tug who took the tow from us.

Later we were told the device was harmless but it was the first of its kind. It had probably been damaged by one of our inshore sweepers and only surfaced later. Anyway, it gave us some excitement in our dull existence.

Winter came and there was no change in our operations, except that it was colder. We had a new Senior Officer whom no one respected. If the weather looked at all rough, affecting our sweeping, he would call off the whole day's sweep without even going to sea to check the weather in our operational area. He had a mistress, Frances Day, a comedy actress of some fame (or notoriety) and some of us irreverently believed he preferred remaining in bed with her to sailing out in the early dawn to sweep mines. He was a retired officer who had been 'on the beach' for some years before being called up again so perhaps he was missing his creature comforts.

It had now been over a year since that day in Dumbarton when a raw crew came on board and now they were a hardened minesweeper outfit. It was time for change and the most important was a change of Captain. Ticky Malins was appointed to a destroyer, which was what he wanted. I was sorry to see him go. We had taken the ship out of the builders' yard together and had trained our 'green' crew in the art of safe minesweeping. He had been a fine example to me – strong on discipline but absolutely fair. Changing Captains is never easy for the second in command. I had got used to Ticky Malins' ways and we came out of the same Dartmouth cocoon and knew what to expect of each other. The new

Captain was a Royal Naval Reserve officer from the merchant navy. A fine seaman but we didn't hit it off. My fault I expect. I have never liked change.

Towards the end of 1941 the Germans began making extensive use of acoustic mines, which exploded on the seabed beneath you when they heard you coming. The countermeasure was to fit all sweepers with a huge electrically operated hammer inside a steel box in the bows below the waterline so that it made a loud noise that rippled out ahead of the ship and blew the mine up safely before the sweeper reached it. We were 'hammered' in Portsmouth Dockyard during a short refit.

We went into dry dock near HMS *Victory*, Nelson's flagship, at Trafalgar. We couldn't have chosen a worse time to go into dock, right in the middle of the blitz on Portsmouth, where the priority targets were the railway station and the dockyard. The Germans had adopted the technique of attacking the same city night after night to swamp the air raid defences and much of the city and the dockyard had been flattened. The bombers would come over after dark on the moonlight nights and drop thousands of incendiary bombs to set the buildings alight and provide a marker for the heavy bombers later. When the city was well alight they dropped land mines and heavy bombs.

The din was appalling; bombs exploding nearby mixed in with the crack of our own anti-aircraft fire – a hellish cacophony. Being in dry dock made it worse for us as we lost the protection of the sea around us and there was nothing for us to do. Guns can't be fired in dry dock as gunfire would damage the ship's hull. We didn't even have an air raid shelter to go to as we had to stay on board to put out any fires, but we only had a skeleton crew on board as the rest were on leave and I was the only officer.

Of all my war experiences the Portsmouth blitz was one of the most frightening and it made me admire the fire and ambulance crews who went on working night after night in the face of these dreadful attacks. At least they had something to do. It also brought home to me the strains that Londoners and the citizens of other large cities had to endure, not once but repeatedly.

As soon as the sirens wailed I went up on the bridge out of habit and because I could communicate with most places from there. I have never been so petrified as I sat in the Captain's chair with nothing to do except listen to the whistle of the falling bombs and wonder where they were going to land; followed shortly by a salvo of mighty explosions and another dockyard building going up in flames, expecting every minute that it would be our turn next.

The raids went on for several nights and then stopped as the moon waned. During these raids the citizens of Portsmouth, except the old and the civil defence workers, used to traipse out of the city every night on foot and on bicycles and mass on the Portsdown hills and in the suburbs, where they were comparatively safe. The dockyard suffered a lot of damage. Miraculously the ship was unscathed though bombs fell within one hundred yards. The hull was somewhat protected because the ship was sitting in the bottom of a dry dock and her hull was just below the level of the top of the dock.

I knew my time was coming to an end as I had been in *Bridlington* for fifteen months and it was time to move on, to a command I hoped. Soon it was Christmas and we were allowed to give leave to as many of the crew as could be spared, including me.

At home in Belstone time seemed to have stood still. War still had not touched it and the rural life carried on undisturbed. In the pub I was regaled with an amazing war story.

'Tony, did you know a cow was killed in Sticklepath?' Sticklepath was a village a mile away. What a horror! Apparently a German bomber returning from a raid on Bristol had unloaded his spare bombs and one of them had destroyed the unfortunate cow. This was the extent of war devastation in our part of Devon. The Christmas break was lovely for a few days' rest but as always it unsettled me. The contrast between such peacefulness and absence of danger seemed unnatural in the midst of our life and death struggle. After two years at sea open to attacks from the air, the sea and under the sea most of us had adjusted to the normality of life in wartime. It had become routine and we went about our business without worry or fear. It was only when we encountered life as it had once been in peacetime that our defences were attacked. This unease always seemed to afflict me whenever I enjoyed time ashore and I never overcame it. As soon as I got back on board such weakness disappeared.

Then the bomb dropped, not a real one, but a letter of appointment to HMS *Mercury*, the naval signal school near Petersfield in Hampshire. There was to be no ship and no command. I was bitterly disappointed as some of my Drake term mates already had commands. Nor did I feel happy to be sitting ashore when I ought to be at sea.

I only had six weeks left in *Bridlington* and after the Christmas leave I had to take the duty over the New Year while the other officers went on leave. Thus while half the crew were living it up ashore I was stuck on board for the birth of 1942. I couldn't complain as I had had the Christmas leave period, but I was bored to the bone. The men onboard must have sensed this, as most of the duty watch turned up outside my cabin after supper and they had obviously got at the rum and had brought me rum 'sippers'. This is a naval term when offering someone a share of your drink. It was all highly irregular and I ought to have come down heavy with them and sent them packing, but I knew them very well by now and I felt I could trust them to behave. So a New Year's Eve party started. I should say that the ship was still immobilised and could not go to sea and we only had to put out fires if there was an air raid.

I felt I ought to contribute to the party by providing some bottles from the wardroom wine store on my account. A noisy sing song took us to Auld Lang Syne, much handshaking and good wishes and they melted happily away. There were no casualties and I wasn't court-martialled because nobody heard of this breach of naval discipline as I was the Duty Officer.

I had a few final weeks steaming up and down the Channel sweeping both for'd and aft with the old wires and the new hammer, and following the same old routine I had grown used to in the last two and a half years in *Skipjack* and *Bridlington*. I had survived and, strangely, enjoyed much of my time in both ships. Danger had only popped up in small doses, intense at the time, but soon forgotten. A little spice to leaven the long days of boring minesweeping, although I wouldn't have thought that if I had been maimed or killed.

It had been particularly satisfying to watch the very young, raw group that had piled out of the train in Glasgow fifteen months before grow in stature and confidence. These two and a half years in *Skipjack* and *Bridlington* had also given me confidence that I could face danger without showing fear and this was to stand me good stead for the rest of the war. I was still only twenty-two.

It may seem strange that, in the midst of war, I could be so happy in my little minesweeper. But I was. I had watched her being built: I had been there when we marched the new Ship's Company on board and the day we had commissioned another of His Majesty's ships, rather like a father with his first baby.

Commissioning a brand new ship is a unique experience. If you join a regiment it has been around for a long time and has its own special traditions. A new ship is like a fresh canvas waiting for the picture to be painted on it. The ship and its role imposes its own character on its inhabitants. You don't see her as an inanimate object but as a living being with quirks and virtues and faults all of her own. One comes to have a great affection for this grey mistress.

We hadn't swept many mines but, more important, we had made sure that the channels for our convoys bringing vital supplies for the war effort were safe. The companionship with such a diverse crew of officers and men had been rewarding. Being a small ship I had got to know the rest of the crew as well as my sweeping team, the engineers, the signalmen and radio operators. We had not lost a single man nor had any been seriously injured. This gave me a great sense of satisfaction.

And always there had been the mighty ocean, beautiful and magnificent, at times horrifying; grey when the black clouds covered the sky; blue in the sunshine; white when the stormy waves broke over the little ship from stem to stern.

On my last night the Ship's Company invited me for a farewell drink in a local pub on the Hard at Portsmouth. I managed to walk back on board without assistance, much to the disappointment of the crew.

The next day the Captain arranged a short parade on the quarterdeck and I was presented by the Ship's Company with a silver tankard, which I still use sixty-eight years later. Of course I had to say something. I burbled away with the usual banalities – great ship, wonderful crew, happy times, miss you all, and in fact it was true. I said goodbye and left. Early next morning I crept out of bed in the Keppel's Head hotel and watched from the window as my ship sailed out of harbour, the first time without me. Farewell to a happy fifteen months.

As I sat alone in my hotel room and reflected on the two and a half years I had spent in minesweepers as Navigator and First Lieutenant it seemed an extraordinary experience. At the start apprehension as to what lay ahead, expecting danger and having to confront inner fears, followed by many peaceful days at sea although the mines lurked beneath. Then the fears and dangers disappeared and boredom became the hazard. Most of the time we didn't dwell on the risks except when, out of a clear blue sky, hell broke loose and we thought we might be about to die. But these were brief spasms soon forgotten and they did perk everybody up.

But there was a need for constant vigilance when sweeping, when one careless moment could result in the ship being blown up. This vigilance demanded a high standard of seamanship from the seamen on the sweep deck and they could see how important it was. This bred a real spirit of teamwork when working the sweeps and a close relationship between myself and the crew, which I much enjoyed.

In those class-conscious days a regular naval officer, trained at the Royal Naval College, was accorded great respect by sailors, which he only lost if he didn't measure up. If he lost it he hardly ever regained it. I too had a considerable respect for our Ship's Company who lived under fairly basic conditions on crowded messdecks with no privacy and slept in hammocks slung above the table where they ate their meals, which they had to prepare themselves. Yet they remained cheerful and ready for a joke even when life was grim.

It hadn't been a glamorous, action-packed couple of years. There had been no exciting clashes with enemy ships or submarines. There had been nothing to write home about, but *Skipjack* and *Bridlington* had helped to keep the convoy routes safe for the merchant ships bringing home all the supplies needed to fight the war. I felt quietly satisfied with my small part.

Chapter Seven

Brief Respite

The Signal School

The signal had read 'Report to HMS *Mercury*, Leydene House, East Meon, Petersfield at 1200 on 15th February'. This was the day after I left *Bridlington*. No leave. I was to become a specialist signal officer, somewhat against my will. I would rather be Captain of a ship. I had not volunteered for this specialisation and felt I would be out of place in this rarefied atmosphere of the signal world, whose mentor was the Earl Mountbatten. Naval gossip had it that you always wore silk ties and had to have a cream-coloured handkerchief peeping out of your breast pocket. Polo, huntin' and shootin' were the preferred pastimes of the pukka signal officer – none of which I indulged in and even disliked. I was also much the youngest student in the class and felt I had little in common with my class mates. In fact, the gossip was hopelessly out of date and my class mates turned out to be delightful, including one old friend who had been captain of my first dormitory at my preparatory school.

I was met at Petersfield station by a lovely Wren driver and a white van and taken to Leydene House. She filled me in with a lot of information about the set-up as we drove along. I was deposited outside an imposing front entrance to a country mansion, dominating the hillside of the South Downs above East Meon. It seemed rather inappropriate when we were desperately struggling at sea in the fraught Battle of the Atlantic. The battle was not going our way and our merchant seamen were suffering losses.

The reason for this gracious living was that the naval signal school in the dockyard at Portsmouth had been bombed out and all the specialist schools had been dispersed around the countryside of South Hampshire to avoid being bombed again. Leydene House had belonged to the Peel family, not ancient landed gentry, but solid money made in the manufacture of linoleum. When the Captain of the signal school arrived to tell Lady Peel that the Royal Navy had to requisition the property the butler informed her 'The men from the dockyard are here Madam'.

Lady Peel was reluctant to leave her mansion but in wartime the authorities had the power to requisition almost anything. So poor Lady Peel was turfed out. I believe she had other residences.

The Hall Porter escorted me to my room, the Bamboo Room, about three times the size of my cabin in *Bridlington*, with glorious views across Hampshire to the sea in the Solent and the Isle of Wight in the far distance. With my binoculars I imagined I could see our minesweepers working off the island and felt that was where I ought to be, not swanning around in this luxurious honey pot.

It didn't take me long to enjoy the change and feelings of guilt soon dissolved. It was the first time since 1939 that I was able to enjoy an almost normal social life. Women abounded; the signal specialisation had been thrown open to the ladies at the start of the war. Several of them were students on courses similar to mine. Female coders, radio operators and signallers were being trained to take over the shore stations and release the men for seagoing service. My future wife had just competed her training as a cipher officer but once again we sailed past each other and never met. Like all those called up for war service she had started at the bottom of the ladder as an ordinary signalman at the age of eighteen and worked her way up to Third Officer, Women's Royal Naval Service.

The daughter of an old friend of my mother's at Bexhill had been called up and was training at the school. An alumnus of a prestigious private girls' school that educated girls to be genteel young ladies suitable for marriage, she had been pitched into the hurly burly of life on the lower deck amongst the rough tars, or so her mother feared. I was asked to find out how she was faring and report back to the anxious mother. Eventually I located her at a Ship's Company dance, tightly embraced by a young signalman and obviously having the time of her life. Certainly I was *de trop* and mumbled my greetings and left the two youths to their amours. I reported back to her mum that her daughter had settled down well and that she was in good hands. I didn't say whose.

The subjects on my course didn't interest me: radio theory and practice, flag signalling and other methods of visual signalling like semaphore. The only one that gripped me at all was the tactical handling of a fleet, known as fleetwork. My heart was not in my learning and this showed in my exam results where I came second from bottom. It all seemed so remote from the sea war and the rough and ready months spent sweeping mines. I paid one visit to my old ship when she was in Portsmouth and checked in at the wardroom but there were several new officers whom I did not know and I also went for'd to the seamen's messdeck to see some of my old minesweeping team, but one should never go back. You can't replicate the past. I played no part in their lives now and after the inevitable badinage about my 'cushy number' ashore I left. I never went back again.

It was a 'cushy number' except that it was hard work getting back to the books again after six years and it showed how rusty my brain had become.

I mustn't exaggerate the down side of this signal course because there were many plusses – summer evenings on the terrace drinking with charming Wren officers and enjoying the beauty of the South Downs, laid out before us. There was plenty of sport, tennis and squash and desperate games of croquet. Situated as we were on a high ridge of the Downs there were some magnificent walks along these lovely hills. Since living on Dartmoor I had come to appreciate hill walking and I had some fine long distance hikes at weekends, which took my mind off classroom boredom. Some weekends I was able to escape to my home on Dartmoor.

Despite these pleasures I was ready, by November, to 'go down to the sea again, to the lonely sea and the sky and a grey mist on the sea's face and grey dawn breaking' (Masefield).

Chapter Eight

Thrills

Hunting

After two weeks' 'end of course' leave I joined HMS *Mendip*, a modern Hunt Class destroyer based at Sheerness, or Sheernasty as the sailors called it, a second rate naval base in the Thames Estuary. *Mendip* and five others of her class had been given the job of defending the east coast convoys against E-boat attack. These fast German torpedo craft carried torpedoes and light guns and were based at Ijmuiden fifty miles away on the Dutch coast. They used to nip across the North Sea under cover of darkness and attack the ships in convoy with their torpedoes. We were suffering significant casualties as the outward bound convoys left the shelter of the Thames estuary or the home bound ships just before they arrived after their journey of thousands of miles.

My new job was completely different from my recent minesweeping duties. I was now a staff officer, responsible for the signal communications in all six ships of our flotilla. Apart from standing my watch on the bridge I had no ship's duties, so I had little interaction with the Ship's Company except for my signalmen and radio operators. The Captain of the ship, Cecil Parry, a four stripe captain, commanded the whole flotilla and I was responsible to him. While I missed the close contact with the Ship's Company that I had enjoyed in *Skipjack* and *Bridlington* my work was much more interesting and, rather grudgingly, I appreciated the training I had suffered at the Signal School.

The role of a destroyer such as *Mendip* was a complete contrast to the passive function of a minesweeper. *Mendip* was fast, aggressive, a hunter and life at sea was exciting. She could speed at 25 knots, nearly 30 mph. We had a lively and interesting wardroom of young regular and reserve officers and our youngish Captain was a fine leader and amusing raconteur.

We hunted by night, prowling in the darkness to pick up on our radar the small echoes that revealed the E-boats. We were greatly helped by our 'Headache' operators. 'Headache' was the top-secret code name for fluent German speakers, men who were really civilians, but wore naval uniforms to protect them from reprisals if they were captured. Some of them were actually Germans, Jews who had escaped their persecution in Germany before the war, and very vulnerable if they were caught.

Our 'Headache' operators, for whom I was responsible, listened in on special radio receivers tuned in to the E-boat frequencies and translated and reported their signals and conversations to the bridge. For some extraordinary reason the E-boat captains were great chatterers and as soon as they left Ijmuiden we picked up their chat. Often they were boasting of their exciting run ashore and encounters with some local beauties.

'She was gorgeous, very willing and I shall see her again.' And other more vivid and erotic stories of sexual conquest. This chatter stopped as they moved out into the open sea and then we became interested in their manoeuvring signals and the description of what they were aiming to do. 'Headache' could give us their direction (bearing) but not their distance (range) and this gave us a good idea of their point of attack on the convoy. We could then adjust our position to meet the threat and lie in wait to seaward of the convoy. This would give us a chance to intercept the enemy before they were in range of the ships.

The convoy was not an easy target to protect as it could be ten miles long from head to tail. Our radar would be the first to pick up the enemy, giving the Captain the range and bearing of the E-boats. After the initial radar contacts it was more Hollywood than North Sea. As soon as the E-boats came within extreme range the Captain would order 'Open fire with starshell'. These burst high up in the sky and came floating slowly down casting an eerie green light over a wide area of the face of the sea. If the radar could give an accurate range and bearing the forward guns would be ordered to open fire by radar. Meanwhile, everyone on the bridge was searching for the small dark shapes lurking somewhere. It was vital to open fire before they could disappear into the night or fire their torpedoes at us.

'Three E-boats bearing green two zero,' shouted the starboard lookout. That is twenty degrees off the starboard bow.

'HE bearing green one zero, getting louder,' from the hydrophone operator. This told us that the enemy had fired torpedoes and they were approaching us. Hydrophones could pick up the direction of the propeller noise of a torpedo but could not give an accurate range.

Signal to the flotilla: 'Torpedoes green one zero. Comb tracks.'

All eyes on the bridge looked for the telltale torpedo tracks, sometimes easy to see if there is luminosity on the sea surface.

'Starboard twenty,' from the Captain to the wheelhouse and we watched the track pass harmlessly down our port side. In the meantime any ship in the flotilla that could range on the E-boats would open fire with all their guns, but often they had vanished at forty knots before our gunfire took effect. But we had disrupted their attack. They were much faster than us and it was no use chasing them. The action was fast moving and it was over in less than ten minutes. E-boats never hung around once we opened fire as they were extremely vulnerable to our big guns. One hit by a 4-inch shell might ignite their fuel tanks and they would explode.

In early 1942 the Navy nearly pre-dated women serving in warships at sea by some forty years as there were many female 'Headache' operators in shore bases and there was a scarcity of male operators at sea. There was a formidable lady Staff Signal Officer on the shore Commander in Chief's staff and she wanted to send the ladies to sea and we wanted to receive them, but their Lordships of the Admiralty decided this was too adventurous.

Destroyer life was far more exciting than minesweeping and also most satisfying. Whipping signals around fast was an important element in a successful E-boat action. We fine-tuned the speed and efficiency of our signal systems and I felt a real sense of achievement when our Captain told me I had raised the standard of signalling throughout the flotilla. Just as I had bedded happily down in *Mendip* a thunderbolt fell from on high, well actually from their Admiralty Lordships.

'Lieutenant A.G. McCrum is to report forthwith to HMS ... a shore establishment at Largs in Scotland.' I protested to the Captain; the Captain protested to the Commander in Chief but I was told to get on with it and not argue. I had only been in the ship three months and was making my mark. With great regret I had to go.

Chapter Nine

Trepidation

Combined Operations

I had much enjoyed my short destroyer time and I did not thrill to the idea of becoming an amphibious assault specialist, trained for army/navy landings on enemy coasts. I had never fancied leaping out of landing craft to be met by a hail of bullets and having to stick a bayonet into some wretched German's stomach. I recalled our midshipmen's bayonet training – lunge, twist, withdraw and repeat – but I never thought I would have to do it.

My appointment was to the Combined Operations Training Centre, near Largs on the lower reaches of the Firth Of Clyde, familiar territory from *Bridlington* days. There, soldiers, sailors and airmen were trained with the skills needed for an assault on defended enemy beaches. Sailors learned to be soldiers and soldiers learned to be sailors.

Largs was on the east coast of the Firth on a bitterly cold and blustery shore. The Training Centre was on an even bleaker part of the coast north of the town. In February 1943 it was as bleak as the war news. The Japanese had overrun most of South-East Asia in 1942, including the capture of our great naval base at Singapore where 80,000 British servicemen surrendered to the Japanese. They were now threatening Australia. The German army was deep into the Russian homeland. In the Atlantic the convoy losses from the U-boats were still mounting and the Battle of the Atlantic was far from won. Had we succumbed to the U-boat menace we would have been defeated. This would have left America and Russia to contain the Germans and Japanese and thousands of Britons would have been sent to the concentration camps by the invading German armies.

Looking back to those days I am surprised how little we were concerned with the big wide world beyond our limited horizon. We trained hard and it was unfamiliar and interesting and we had no time to worry about the wider war.

At least in the Middle East General Montgomery in November 1942 had defeated the Afrika Korps at El Alamein and was advancing westwards while the Americans and a new British 1st Army had landed in Morocco and Algeria in

Operation *Torch*. I quickly realised we were slotted in for an assault landing in Europe later on in 1943.

After a few weeks of lectures, leaping in and out of landing craft and setting up beach organisations on 'captured' beaches we were deemed fit for the fray. I was still somewhat apprehensive about my next job. Would it be leading a Beach Signal Station team in the assault waves or organising the signals of a squadron of landing ships? War certainly gave one variety – minesweepers, destroyers, and now assault landings. I would never have had such variety or so many thrills in the peacetime Navy.

After the course was over my next appointment came through and it was rather an anti climax. 'You are appointed to HMS *Largs* as Signal Officer in Charge.'

What on earth was *Largs*, certainly not the town near the Combined Operations Centre. Her name did not appear in the Navy List of HM Ships. She was a West Indies banana boat that had been converted into a Headquarters Ship (Landing Ship, Headquarters, LSH) full of radio and radar equipment and was designed to communicate with and control an army division and squadrons of landing ships and aircraft. She was just a box full of specialised operations rooms and signal equipment, a floating headquarters for the Admiral and General commanding a landing from which they would be able to control all the forces in the early days of an assault. It turned out to be a fascinating appointment but I didn't know that then.

So, after all, I would not be required to stick bayonets into German soldiers and my main task was to weld a group of RAF, Army and Navy signallers into a skilled inter-service communications team. We had plenty of time as we had to steam all round Africa to get to the Mediterranean, which was still closed to shipping due to enemy air attacks. It was a novel appointment and it turned out to be rewarding and most interesting. There was just enough inter-service rivalry to keep everyone on their toes without any ill feeling. We had a great team and in due course they delivered the goods at the invasion of Sicily, but that was still months ahead. *Largs* was in dock up the Clyde in Greenock and we were able to get to know each other before we sailed. The army and RAF signal officers were a bright bunch, young and eager, and we occasionally led each other astray.

One Sunday after a good lunch some of us decided to climb the hills above Greenock and enjoy a farewell glimpse of the lovely Firth of Clyde as we were sailing the next day. We found ourselves high above the Clyde in glorious sunshine full of *joie de vivre* and gin. One of our group, not me I'm sure, suddenly shouted out 'Pale faces in the valley. We ambush them.' We decided we were Indian braves and followed our leader down the hillside. Soon we were all dashing down the hill hollering as we thought Indian braves should. Unfortunately, we had not realised we were approaching the Greenock golf course, full of Sunday golfers, until some irate golfers shouted at us, 'Bloody disgraceful. You should be fighting the war.'

It was such a lovely day we roared on down the fairway until we were well clear of the course and any pursuit. Juvenile, ridiculous, bad manners, stupid? Yes, all of these, but it was exhilarating charging down the hillside stirring up the solid burghers of Greenock. After that activity we felt on top of the world and by the time we reached the ship we were as sober as judges.

The next day *Largs* sailed down the Clyde to join up with a massive convoy sailing to Egypt via Cape Town. This convoy carried thousands of soldiers and equipment needed for the first invasion of Europe. *Largs* was not really a warship and she formed part of the convoy, not the escort. This was the worst time to be sailing in convoy. The German U-boat campaign was at its height and our Atlantic losses were unsustainable, but we had a large number of naval escorts and hoped they would deter the subs. I had never sailed in a convoy before and I found this passive role unnerving.

Sailing down the Clyde in convoy is a memorable sight. Ships, like a flock of birds, dispersed over the wide estuary, then gradually formed up into strict formation like Canada geese. The escorts fussed round the edges, chasing up the laggards until a disciplined army of shipping moved in stately progression into the open sea. One may be slightly apprehensive about the future but the magnificent Scottish background of mountains and green fields puts any fears out of mind. When would we see England and Scotland again?

Unfortunately for *Largs* when we got out into the Atlantic we completely broke down and lay wallowing in the swell and that is the worst thing that can happen to a ship in convoy. She has to be left to fend for herself. From the signals I had decoded I knew there were a number of German subs in our general area so I made sure I knew where my lifebelt was. We had an unpleasant hour stopped while the engineers repaired the machinery but we were a sitting duck for any U-boat. The mending done, we cracked on at speed to get back inside the convoy's protective screen. It was a nasty couple of hours.

During our long journey south we tried to guess where we would be landing. In the evenings we would sit on deck, gazing at the bright starlit sky and ruminate as to our future. Sardinia, Sicily, Greece? Wherever it was to be we were thrilled to be part of it, because at last we were advancing. Moving back into Europe. For over three years we had hung on by a slender thread avoiding defeat. Now we were on the move. The dolphins seemed to be egging us on as they raced alongside the ship and cavorted across our bows but always avoiding them. In the luminous southern seas they were breathtakingly beautiful and hurried us on. Night after night after supper in a stuffy dining room down below decks we enjoyed the cooler air on deck and put the world to rights as one only can in one's twenties.

By day we carried out endless 'paper' exercises to get the international signals 'watches' used to handling large volumes of messages. After a time they palled and we longed for a spot of action.

A short stopover in Freetown was a relief and some friends and I walked along the shore and through a native village, where we were greeted by the whole population, and found ourselves on miles of sandy beach that looked as if it went all the way to Cape Town. I wished I had my surf board and we had a refreshing swim.

Then on to Cape Town, actually Simon's Town a nearby naval base. My only memory of our stay is bananas. There had been no bananas in England since the war began and here they were cheap and plentiful. We swam, we ate bananas; we swam again and ate more bananas and so it went on. Why we didn't get dysentery I don't know but it was fantastic.

Off again to sea and boredom was setting in. However much we tried to vary our paper exercises it was difficult to keep up interest. We tried quizzes and quotations competitions and devised deck games. They helped but we needed some action to sharpen us up.

Up through the Red Sea, which was appallingly hot, with no air conditioning then. I slept on deck as life below in our double cabin was insufferable. At last after a month we reached the Suez Canal and the end of our odyssey. The last time I had passed through the canal I was three years of age, but I could still distinctly remember our P&O liner, on its way to Hong Kong, steaming slowly down this narrow waterway and watching a caravan train of camels walking sedately along the western bank silhouetted by the setting sun, which turned the desert into a sea of gold and then a sinister black. These were my earliest memories and now we were going the other way and back to the war.

At the end of the canal we anchored at Port Said and our Admiral, who had flown out from the UK, welcomed us with his staff. He sent for me.

'McCrum, you are to join my planning staff for Operation *Husky* [code name for the invasion]. Be ready to come back with us to Cairo tomorrow.'

There was little time to look around in Cairo and no tourist visit to the Sphinx. Soon we were on our way to Algeria in a rather basic American aircraft, known as a DC10. Hard metal seats and no air hostesses. Endless brown sands below us where much British, Australian, South African and New Zealand blood had been spilled. Not forgetting the Italian and German dead.

We were well on our way to Algiers when the aircraft decided it had had enough.

'We have to land at Biskra in the Saharan desert. It's a French Foreign Legion outpost. We have to wait there for some spares to be flown out from Cairo,' said the pilot.

This was the beginning of three very dusty days in this insignificant desert town, guarded by a typical Foreign Legion fort as seen in countless Beau Geste

Hollywood films. The spares arrived and we were soon on our way to an air base near Algiers. From there we went by car to Djidjelli, our base port. At this stage of the war Algeria was still a French colony, supposedly governed by the collaborationist Vichy government in France, but the Allies had installed their own man in Algiers. Djidjelli was a charming coastal resort with a tree-lined promenade along the length of the fine harbour, protected by artificial breakwaters. In the background magnificent mountains rose high above us and seemed to overshadow us, although they were some miles inland. The harbour would soon be filled with landing ships and smaller craft allotted to our invasion force. We were billeted in a delightful hotel on the edge of the countryside just outside the town.

On our first morning our small staff foregathered in our harbourside office for the Admiral and his Chief of Staff to brief us. We were the restricted staff who were allowed to be told where our landing was to be and the date and time of the assault. This was called the XO staff and I never discovered what XO stood for; it was obviously terribly secret. We were forbidden to talk about our plans except when we were inside the office. Our assault was to be near Capo Pachino on the south eastern tip of Sicily. D-Day was to be 10 July. I came away from the meeting feeling quite elevated that I, a junior Lieutenant, had been included amongst the select few who knew the score. The future looked really exciting and far more glamorous than I had feared in that dismal training camp at Largs.

It was now late April 1943 and the last German soldier had been chased out of North Africa by General Montgomery's Eighth Army. Now we could reopen the Mediterranean to shipping. For many months the central Med had been closed due to the ferocity of the enemy air attacks and reinforcements for the Eighth Army had had to trundle all the way round the Cape of Good Hope, as we had recently endured.

We had less than two months to plan our assault and no sooner had we begun than Monty threw a spanner in the works and demanded a rewrite of the overall plan. The American, British and Canadian armies were to land along the coast of southern Sicily in a chain of assaults supporting each other. Monty thought the landings were too far apart for mutual support and demanded that they should be more concentrated. He was probably right but finding new beaches and laying out fresh convoy lanes took time. Luckily our landing was unaffected by the changes and we were able to get on with our plans.

Our full staff was tri-service, Army, Navy and Air Force, all British, and we all ate and drank together, surely one of the reasons for our future success. Many a minor inter-service snag could be settled at the bar and we were soon 'all of one company'. By contrast the Americans, at that time, still suffered from intense inter-service rivalry and hardly spoke to each other.

The harbour filled up with a vast array of landing ships and smaller craft of every description. *Largs* was there, tank landing ships, cross channel ferries converted to carry assault craft, landing craft fitted with a bombarding gun and landing craft carrying hundreds of explosive rockets that fired off within a minute, useful for blowing up mines under the sand.

Apart from helping my boss to plan the communications for our force my main task was to train the beach signals parties and the landing ships and craft into an inter-connecting signal system for a successful landing. *Largs* was the centre of an intricate web of communication channels that enabled the Admiral and the General to control this complex military operation.

The soldiers we would be landing were Scotsmen of the 51st Highland Division, battle hardened after fighting their way across the deserts of Egypt, Libya and Tunisia. They were a tough bunch, rather arrogant and self-assured and fine fighting men. Now they had to learn how to live on board a ship and storm ashore on hostile beaches after feeling seasick. A happy marriage between landing craft crews and soldiers was important and training soon began. The Highland Division had had a rough time and suffered many casualties from mines in the sands of the desert.

Our first major challenge came when the General told the naval staff, 'I don't want the assault waves to land on a sandy beach.'

Where else could they land? How about flat rocks. The Navy usually tries to avoid rocks like the plague; they're very unfriendly to ships' bottoms. It had never been done before but our two beaches had some flattish rocks on one side. Rock landings were a novelty and we accepted the challenge.

Selecting our best assault craft flotillas they started training on some local rocks and it was found that if the craft approached very slowly and steadily it could be done but it was hazardous. Throughout June training went on relentlessly. The ships, the soldiers and the supporting aircraft had to be woven into a complicated tapestry with every strand in exactly the right position. Further along the coast to the west of us other British, American and Canadian assault forces were also testing their plans.

The armies were to land on a strip of the southern coast of Sicily with the Americans striking west towards Palermo and the British pushing north to Catania. Some 100,000 men, with their guns, tanks, ammunition and stores, would be storming across the landing beaches. In the meantime the soldiers had to be trained in assault techniques so that when H hour came they would rush out of the bow doors into the shallow waters (we hoped) and up the beach. Each landing craft had bow doors that opened to allow a ramp to be lowered on to the sand like modern car ferries. The Navy had to learn how to manoeuvre these unwieldy craft and get them as far up the beach as possible so that the soldiers had a dry landing and the craft would not be stranded on the beach.

Largs took part in this training to test the communications that would enable the Admiral and the General to issue orders to their ships and their troops and to receive orders from the Supreme Allied Commander, General Eisenhower, and the Naval Commander in Chief, ashore in Malta. General Eisenhower was in overall charge of all naval, army and air forces and Admiral Cunningham, a British Admiral, commanded all the naval forces. With the Air Commander in Chief they were located in a headquarters ashore in Malta.

As D-Day drew nearer we were busy from dawn to dusk and I went to sea in all sorts of ships and craft that were practising landings on a nearby beach. Ships usually returned to harbour in the evening and I always tried to get some exercise after the day's work was over. Our hotel was close to open country and I would walk the lanes in the dusk to get a few moments' peace away from it all. I have always felt the need to escape the pressures of the day on my own. The enemy aircraft raided the harbour intermittently in the evenings but caused little damage.

July came and the inter-service staffs went on board *Largs* with the Admiral Rhoddy McGrigor, and General Wimberley, the Assault Commanders. We were ready for the off and we carried out a complete dress rehearsal on our practice beaches to iron out any remaining wrinkles.

Chapter Ten

Anticipation

Operation *Husky*

Sfax was the jumping off point for many of the assault ships and the whole of our particular group. We trundled along the North African coast and spent a few days in Sfax to make our final preparations. On the eve of departure there was a D-Day briefing. We assembled in a huge cinema to brief the D-Day assault teams with the Admiral and General and their planning staffs on the stage and the massed ranks of Commanding Officers of Landing Ships and Craft, Company Commanders of the assault troops and other military and air force officers facing them in the auditorium. This was the final pre-op briefing before the assault convoys sailed in forty-eight hours' time. The tension in the hall was palpable as they waited to hear where and when they were going to land. We were all apprehensive as to what lay ahead in this the first major assault since the disaster at Gallipoli in World War I.

There was complete silence as the planners outlined the details of the landing during the night on two beaches on the Sicilian coast and the enemy intelligence. There were possible minefields; Italian army units in the vicinity but no Germans; and German and Italian air attacks were expected. Naval opposition was an unknown quantity but the most likely opposition was from motor torpedo boats and submarines.

The audience was all hyped up after hearing the details of the plan, anticipating a defended coastline, mines in the sand, troops dug in behind the sand dunes and bombers overhead. Then two young naval officers were ushered on to the stage by the Admiral who introduced them as members of a Special Boat Section. This was a top secret commando unit that was landed on enemy coasts to spy out the land or carry out special missions.

These two young men had just arrived back from our assault beaches. They were so young they looked like school leavers. They may have been young but they gave a completely assured briefing.

'We have spent the last week in and around Red and Green beaches and both beaches are clear of mines and there are no underwater obstructions offshore. We have walked round the foreshore several times and we found no gun emplacements or fortifications.'

As a parting shot their leader added with a grin 'It's really rather a pleasant spot'.

The audience was transfixed. These guys had been wandering around in the assault area for several days. The tension in the audience drained away. Everyone relaxed. And what's more their report was remarkably accurate.

Two days later we put the troops ashore and there was, initially, no opposition and no minefields. I had studied the story of the Gallipoli disaster where the troops were landed from open rowing boats towed by steam picket boats and there were no specialist landing craft. I remembered how sailors and soldiers were mown down by well camouflaged machine-gun fire from the cliffs above. Gallipoli had been a total disaster and after some months clinging to precarious positions our soldiers, many of whom were Australian and New Zealanders, had had to be evacuated. Then in our present war the raid on the French coast at Dieppe by Canadian and British soldiers had also been a costly failure and the photographs of stranded tanks and landing craft on the beach told a grim story. Casualties were heavy and nothing was achieved except that we needed improved landing craft and specialist assault equipment if we were to land successfully on a hostile shore.

The Sicily landing was therefore a leap in the dark. The prospect was exciting but also daunting. During the weeks of planning I appreciated just how much thought had been put into this operation, nothing botched about our plans, rigorously examined by all three services teams. However carefully plans are laid one of the rules of war is to be certain that an operation will never go as planned.

A few days before D-Day I found myself impatient to be off, to see what happened when the curtain went up on the stage at Capo Pachino and I also still had a nagging fear that it might just turn out to be another Gallipoli. I was too busy to really worry much and the excitement we all felt at this unique assault far outweighed any apprehensions we might have.

Now three years after we had been thrown off the continent at Dunkirk we were going back to invade it and we were rearing to go.

A few days after D-Day I wrote a short description of my angle on the assault phase of Operation *Husky*. Reading it now, many years later, it seems rather naïve and some allowance needs to be made for 'battle hyperbole' but it does reflect my feelings at the time and I have not tried to civilise it.

The day of July 8th was waning as we set off in two columns of ships from the North African port of Sfax. A tremendous surge of excitement ran through the ship as this vanguard of the avenging armada steamed quietly out of the bay. Three years, long years they had been, since the Navy had last transported the army, then in the wrong direction. Now the wheels of justice had turned in our favour once more. The Navy was confident that it could hurl our army like some medieval battering ram at the enemy's shore and break his resistance.

The next day produced a freshening north-west wind and the officers on the bridge grew anxious about the prompt arrival of the other convoys of smaller landing craft which were to join us off Malta. So much of our success would depend on the meticulous timing of convoys arriving off the hostile shore. By teatime half a gale was blowing and faces grew longer and longer. It is impossible to beach landing craft safely in a running surf.

However, half an hour later, pounding in from the west, came the first convoy of landing craft carrying hundreds of seasick soldiers. It was a wonderful sight to see row upon row of these little craft smashing through the waves and tearing through them as fast as they could go, while behind them a fiery sun was setting behind the bastion of Malta. One could not help wondering how many of us would see the sun next morning.

The landing craft took up their station astern of the larger troop carriers and we altered course for the south-eastern corner of Sicily. It was dark when we met the last of our particular convoys. This one consisted of slow craft carrying artillery, tanks and larger weapons to support the infantry. Unfortunately the weather was still so bad that these ships were delayed. It was a nasty rough passage and the soldiers were stricken with seasickness, which made them all the keener to get ashore.

As the night grew blacker the wind went down quite suddenly, almost mysteriously. By ten o' clock, with a new moon just rising, the angry white horses had vanished and our great force was lifting quietly to a low swell. Towards midnight the decks crowded with officers and men staring into the darkness ahead to try to catch their first glimpse of Sicily, unaware of its approaching fate. There had not been any sign of the enemy.

Away to the north the RAF was pounding the port of Syracuse and their flares could be clearly seen floating down to earth amidst the coloured tracer from the Italian anti-aircraft guns. But there was still no sign that our foe knew that this vast concourse of shipping was approaching. The peace and quiet of the night was eerie and we could hardly believe that we had surprised them. Yet we had.

At forty minutes after midnight the ships stopped and the larger landing ships lowered their assault craft carrying the first wave of our troops. As their white wakes merged into the night we realised that a long period of anxious waiting lay ahead until we had the first reports of the landing. We watched the low dark line of the coast for signs of resistance, trying hard to pierce the wall of darkness and see what was happening ashore. Then at 2.45 am the signal was flashed back 'Red beach captured' followed shortly by 'Green beach captured'. Our plans were working well.

From time to time reports came in that gave a confused picture of slight resistance and advances inland. At first light *Largs* moved closer inshore to catch a glimpse of what was happening on land. The low coastline, bathed in warm Mediterranean sunshine, was as peaceful as the south coast of England in summer. So quiet was it that it was hard to believe this really was an invasion. Overhead there were no dive-bombers, on the sea no enemy fleet and underwater no submarines. How completely different from those black days at Dunkirk three years earlier.

All day we steamed up and down off the beaches without seeing any sign of the enemy. The advance swept on like some overpowering wave. Throughout the day as far as the eye could see small craft were dashing to and fro from those yellow beaches throwing more and more strength into the battle. All the while the larger ships, huge liners, smaller cross channel ferries, cargo ships, cruisers, destroyers, minesweepers and swarms of small coastal craft lay off the coast either at anchor unloading or cruising up and down in support, bombarding or patrolling against possible U-boats. Enemy aircraft made feeble attempts to prevent the unloading but they were driven off by our Malta-based fighters without doing much harm.

By nightfall we knew we had, at least, secured a valuable bridgehead and one and all felt sure of the ultimate success of this colossal invasion. Everywhere there was a feeling of quiet satisfaction and, I think, pride that after those three years of hammering and battering, which Britain had sustained since June 1940, she was still able to hurl a weight of defiance at our treacherous enemies.

That concluded what I wrote at the time.

The assault had been a fantastic success. There were hardly any casualties amongst the 51st Highland Division landing on the beaches and they advanced rapidly inland against only light opposition. On the morning of D-Day we heard a surprised Italian pilot reporting back to his base.

'There are ships everywhere. Thousands and thousands of ships. The sea is black with them.'

We were, of course, intercepting all the enemy air communications signals. We had expected E-boat, submarine and even surface ship attack but none came and there was no attempt to interfere with our operation. The Italian fleet remained in their bases.

The worst casualties were self inflicted when the paratroopers being dropped inshore of the beaches were landed in the sea. Due to a navigational error about half of them fell into the sea to the east of the beachhead. It was dark and we could hear them calling out for help. Boats were sent but many drowned as they were tangled up in their parachutes. It was a tragedy because the rest of the landing had been so successful. It was so quiet that on D+1, the second day of the assault, I was able to go ashore to visit the beach signal stations and see if they needed anything. When I landed at Green beach it looked more like a sunny day on a Bank Holiday in Blackpool than the focus of an assault landing. Vehicles, guns and equipment were being landed onto the artificial beach roadway but anyone who had nothing to do was bathing in the beautifully clear Mediterranean. This was too good to miss and I stripped off and dived in; it was probably the most welcome swim of my life. It was so contrary to what we had been expecting. Where was the enemy?

We hadn't long to wait. After the first two nights the enemy realised we were in earnest and began regular air attacks on the anchorage after dark in a rather indiscriminate way. Sometimes the bombing came unpleasantly close, probably because we were one of the larger ships in the anchorage. During these attacks we were at 'Action Stations' although there wasn't much we could do. My station was in the middle of the communications centre. Round the sides were ranged the naval, army and RAF radio operators.

To help me set an example of British sangfroid, which I did not feel, I used to take a paperback thriller to read when the bombs started falling. I hoped this would take my mind off the bombing and instinctively ducking under the table. There is always an intense desire to get under cover when enduring an air attack where you can't hit back. As several of the radio operators tried to dive under their desks I did my best to remain upright and studiously reading my book, even if my heart was hammering away like an automatic hammer. These excitements died away after a few days and they were the only occasion when we faced enemy action.

As soon as things began to settle down and the General and his staff had set up their headquarters ashore *Largs* was ordered to Augusta, an Italian naval base just round the corner, which the army had captured. *Largs* was needed as the Port Headquarters until the shore offices were ready.

Augusta had been doubly damaged, by our air raids and the spoiling activities of the retreating enemy. I had to leave the relative comfort of the ship to help set up the shore communications. There was no running water, no sanitation and army field rations, not the tastiest of dishes. It was one of life's great experiences but we were working so hard it didn't bother us unduly. On amphibious operations, as I was to discover later, life was one series of ups and downs, highs and lows. It's what made life such fun. It only lasted a few days for me as I was whisked off to Algiers to plan the next assault at Salerno, near Naples. I was sorry to leave the Admiral's staff as I felt I had been successful. Months later I was 'Mentioned in Despatches' for my time on his staff and five years later the Admiral invited me to be his Flag Lieutenant (sort of PA) so my face must have fitted. I was also sorry to leave our inter-service communications team who had worked so well together and shown they were highly skilled in amphibious communications.

The success of the assault on Sicily by British, American and Canadian forces effectively placed the Mediterranean area firmly under our control. The war in Africa was over.

As I flew over the Mediterranean to Algiers I looked back on the last few months. Up to then my war experiences had been standard naval fare, minesweepers and destroyers in their traditional roles. The combined operations experience was novel, unusual and most interesting with bouts of intense excitement.

It had been illuminating to work so closely with members of the other services and to understand more about military and air operations. It gave me a new and much less insular outlook on service life. I had learned much about the problems and thinking of the army and had glimpses of how senior officers controlled the battle. This gave me a fresh outlook on my jobs and I felt ready to tackle new challenges. I had come a long way from the nervousness and diffidence of those early days of the war in *Skipjack* where I had that constant worry that I might let myself down and show fear in the face of the enemy.

Chapter Eleven

Ultra

The Unknown

Algiers was the headquarters of the Supreme Allied Commander, Mediterranean, General Dwight Eisenhower and the British naval Commander in Chief. I found myself considered to be an expert in communications for an assault landing and was given the task of helping to plan the next assault on Italy at Salerno. D-Day was 15 September, less than two months away. Because I was only a temporary member of staff I stayed in a transit dormitory where officers waiting for a ship were accommodated. This was back to boarding school days or even worse, which is saying something. We were about thirty to a dormitory, which consisted of camp beds on a concrete floor in a shed near the docks. There was absolutely no privacy and only one hole in the ground for a lavatory, Arab style. Accuracy of performance was vital otherwise you missed the hole with displeasing consequences. Luckily this purgatory didn't last long and I was shunted off to the United States Navy.

I had arrived at Algiers at the end of July 1943 and at first 'they' didn't seem to know what to do with me. I had two somewhat idle weeks, which I found frustrating. With hindsight I think the naval Commander in Chief's staff did know but couldn't tell me until the positive 'vetting' process for the Ultra signal system had been completed and I was cleared. This vetting was to make sure there were no murky incidents in my past and I was a fit person to handle highly secret intelligence. Fortunately I was whiter than white or any past sins were not uncovered. Then I was indoctrinated into the Ultra system, which handled intelligence emanating from Bletchley Park in Buckinghamshire. Bletchley Park was the headquarters of a most secret organisation that broke into enemy codes. Early on in the war we had discovered how to break the German codes. These were then translated into English and retransmitted to the commanders in the field in a complex cipher. At that time we were regularly decoding most of their important messages and our Admirals and Generals knew what the enemy was planning.

I was to be in charge of a small team of seagoing radio operators who would receive the English version of the Ultra decodes. It was my job to decipher all signals with the Ultra prefix. I then had to take them personally to one or two people who had been cleared to see this intelligence, usually the Admiral and his Chief of Staff.

The Ultra set-up was so secret that I was required to sign a statement that never, ever, would I reveal any of its secrets, not even that it existed or had existed in the past. Shortly after the war I received further written warnings about the secrecy of Ultra and was instructed never to go on holiday to Russia, Poland, Czechoslovakia, Hungary, Bulgaria or Romania, lest I be seduced by some communist houri and enticed to reveal my secrets. What a pity. I had always fancied a bit of seduction but I was not to be tested. Years later I was flabbergasted to read a book by a Group Captain Winterbottom, followed by a detailed TV programme that my wife and I were watching.

'That was what I was doing during the war,' I said

'So was I,' she replied.

At this time the Med was still largely a British command and the strategic communications networks were manned by British naval staffs. It was simpler for all long-range Shore to Ship frequencies to be manned by British radio operators at the ship end. That is what I was to be responsible for in USS *Biscayne*, in charge of a small team of coder ratings, cipher officers and radio operators. This was additional to my personal responsibility for the Ultra intelligence because the Americans had no Ultra capability at this time. This took up much of my time because all Ultra traffic came in an especially secure manual book cipher, which was excessively tedious to decipher. The messages from the Admiralty containing Ultra intelligence were encrypted in what was called the one time pad system. Literally each page of the cipher was only ever used once and only two people held the one time pad in use – the Admiralty and I. As soon as I had deciphered a message the pages from the pad in use were immediately burned. The Germans never realised how much of their most secret plans were in the hands of the Allied Commanders in the field within twenty-four hours.

At the end of August I flew from Algiers to *Bizerte*, a huge French naval base that we had taken over and where the Assault Force was assembling. *Biscayne* was the flagship of Rear Admiral Connelly, USN. He was a splendid man, decisive and very approachable. I got on well with him. His title was COM LAND CRAB NAW, rather a mouthful, which stood for Commander Landing Ships and Craft North Africa West. *Biscayne* was a specially fitted out Headquarters Ship like *Largs* and I felt quite at home. The 5th Army Commander was Lieutenant General Mark Clark who, I thought, was rather vain and weak. These were the two principals that I would be supplying with an Ultra service. I hoped it would be ultra satisfactory.

At this time the British 8th Army under General Montgomery had recently landed on the toe of Italy but was making slow progress up the long Italian instep. Our assault at Salerno was designed to capture the port of Naples quickly and use it as a base to advance north towards Rome.

American ships were magnificently equipped but were uncomfortable to live in. I shared an extremely hot cabin in the bowels of the ship, measuring about eight feet by eight feet. There is no alcohol in US Navy ships so there is none of the RN mess life in the evenings when you can discuss the events of the day and pick holes in your seniors and betters. At meals you had to sit in exactly the same place for all meals with the same neighbours. My right hand neighbour was a mid-westerner with a great interest in growing sorghum wheat but this was the limit of his conversation. The man on my left was a master of the wisecrack, which was more amusing until the third and fourth repetition when it began to pall. It didn't really matter as I was extremely busy and only had time to snatch meals, sleep and work.

Once again the familiar sight of hundreds of landing craft and ships and warships of every description filled the bay. Once again I felt the tingle of excitement that these amphibious assault preparations gave me. There was such a hustle and bustle of last-minute preparations and briefings. Only a few knew exactly when we were sailing and where we were going and everyone was on tenterhooks. I always felt sorry for the soldiers who did not know where they were going nor what reception they might expect on the beaches. At least I knew all the plan details and what to expect. I only wanted to get on with it and see how our plans worked out or didn't.

Biscayne was to be the headquarters ship for the 'Uncle' Attack Group, which was to assault the beaches nearest Salerno and the enemy base.

Admiral Connelly was serving temporarily under the orders of the British Commodore Oliver who commanded the Northern Assault, which was primarily a British military landing. Further south there was a Southern Attack Force, which was an American military landing.

On 6 September at 11.30 hours we slipped from our buoy and moved into the outer bay. As we passed the harbour entrance a British naval honour guard of seamen presented arms while a Royal Marine band played the 'Stars and Stripes'. It was an inspiring little ceremony, which was perfected by the British Port Admiral being there in person to wish us 'God Speed'. Moving out through the vast concourse of shipping we were greeted with a bugle salute as we passed the British cruisers and one and all seemed to be saying 'Good luck; good hunting'.

We remained at anchor in the outer bay as we hoped to slip out of harbour in the dark. There was a wonderful sunset with row upon row of ships and landing craft riding on the face of the sea in sharp relief against the ruddy glow of the dying sun.

Such a throng of shipping could not be concealed from the enemy reconnaissance aircraft for long and at 8.30 pm a powerful force of German bombers did their best to upset our plans but were met with such a concentration of shot and shell that the landing force suffered little damage.

Previously that day we had been thrilled to see squadron after squadron of our own bombers grinding their way across the sky to smash the enemy defences in Italy. There was a high spirit of expectancy on board that night.

D-Day-1, 8 September, was burning hot. Not a rustle of a breeze; the sea a mirror of silver and overhead a brazen sky. We were shadowed by aircraft on and off all morning but no attack developed. At 4.50 pm to our surprise the island of Capri some forty miles away reared its steep cliffs out of the sea. Such was the clarity of the visibility. This meant that our force was also highly visible at a great distance.

A few minutes later the bombing began. It was a long way off, near the slow tank landing craft convoy, and with a sickening heart I watched as *LCT 624* was hit and disappeared in a tower of black smoke and flame rising hundreds of feet into the sky. It was doubtful if there were any survivors. At 6 pm our convoy was attacked but only by a single Messerschmitt dive-bomber that flew down over the screening ships and dropped two small bombs, which just missed an American submarine chaser.

Darkness soon came and calm. There is always something about the eve of an assault that is memorable: the feeling that this huge community of people of every description, spread around in a host of ships over many miles of ocean, are sharing with you that thrilling, awe-inspiring expectancy, of wanting to rip aside dawn's curtain and see what the next day will bring.

On deck, dimly discernible, one can pick out the black ships on all sides and somewhere ahead waits the foe.

That night was unique in all eves of assault for we were to hear that Italy had surrendered and was out of the war – the first of our enemies to be vanquished. As the tannoy announced the news a spontaneous shout of joy echoed throughout our ship and it looked as if the operation would become an occupation.

In fact, it turned out that this armistice announcement confused the execution of the plan in the first hours of the assault. The pre-arranged bombardment of known coastal guns was cancelled and ships were only allowed to open fire if shore guns took action first. The Italians may have surrendered but not the Germans. But above all we relaxed; we thought it would be a walk over. The tension and vigilance had evaporated and we lost concentration, rather like a winning football team that sits back in the last ten minutes, only to see their opponents score winning goals

We had not long to wait before we were disillusioned by inaccurate enemy gunfire, presumably directed by radar on to the assaulting convoys. All we could see in the pitch dark was a distant gleam of light as the guns were fired and about thirty seconds later an explosion. I believe only one tank landing ship was hit.

At daybreak the low-lying sandy coastline gradually emerged from the gloom of the night and from the bridge I could pick out the individual ships with my binoculars – *Mendip*, my old ship, *Blakeney*, *Hilary* and others. It was soon obvious that the army ashore was having a sticky time and their demands for fire support became more and more insistent. All our hopes of an easy landing were quickly blown away and we could see the troops digging in on the beach instead of advancing inland as they had done in Sicily. The destroyers moved close inshore and were firing at almost point blank range at the German Tiger tanks that had broken through to the edge of the beach. The beaches were backed by low trees and scrub and this made concealment easy for the tanks.

From *Biscayne* we could clearly see the fire fight taking place ashore. Smoke, machine-gun fire, artillery and warship bombardment provided a spectacular battle scene such as I had never seen before. It looked like a Hollywood blood and guts film, only men were really dying. In our northern sector the assault had been carried out by the British 46th Division and they were closest to Salerno and the German batteries. It was a touch and go battle for several hours. By nightfall the struggle had turned in our favour but it had been a hard fight with many soldiers killed. The Navy had also taken casualties beaching in the face of heavy machine-gun fire. At one point some US Navy landing ships were heavily shelled as they approached the beach and one or two jibbed at going in. Our Admiral dealt vigorously with this by sending his Chief of Staff in a patrol boat to lead the ships in 'and see that the goddam things stay there till all their load has been landed', which was effectively carried out.

I could only pop up on deck for brief glimpses of the battle as I had my main job to do in the radio office looking after the routine communications to and from the British naval Commander in Chief and the vital Ultra signals from London. Most of the time I was closeted down below in the cipher office. At this stage of the war the Ultra service from Bletchley Park and the Admiralty was brilliant. On the evening of D-Day I deciphered a long signal from the Admiralty, which was a translation of the German Commander's operation orders for the next day, telling us exactly what their plans were and how they were to be carried out. When I presented the deciphered version to the Admiral and the General the latter turned to me and said 'Gee Tony, I don't know how you do it'.

I felt I had to explain that all I did was to decipher the messages that were prepared from intercepted enemy signals at Bletchley Park in England. I had no intelligence role except occasionally interpreting unusual 'Limey' phrases. Our Commanders were receiving the intercepted enemy signals almost as soon as the German formations were. The Ultra system contributed hugely and anonymously to our successes.

After we had landed our assault troops and their equipment *Biscayne* moved to the Southern Attack Area to take charge of the American landing there.

Sometimes when I was decoding an Ultra I got an almighty shock when enemy action against the naval forces was revealed. One evening I began decoding a signal that had been sent from the *Luftwaffe* Headquarters in Italy to one of their air squadrons. The first sentence read 'You are to attack the southern assault anchorage at first light tomorrow'. Fairly standard stuff, but the next few words made me sit up with a start. 'The priority target is the assault flagship.' That was us! Worse was to follow. 'Special Weapon X to be used with setting….' What was Special Weapon X? Some new development in bigger and better bombs?

I took the signal to the Admiral and his Chief of Staff and they discussed what action they could take. One of the golden rules of the Ultra system was that no action could be taken that might reveal that we had broken their ciphers. This severely restricted the counter action we could take. We couldn't just up anchor and sail out to sea and clear the anchorage. That would have been too obvious. The Admiral requested increased air patrols and ships were warned to be particularly alert in the early morning. There was not much more we could do.

Shortly after receiving that Ultra signal we got a message from the Admiralty, marked EMERGENCY, warning us that the Germans might be about to try out a new secret weapon, possibly some sort of radio-guided rocket or bomb. There were no known countermeasures and their somewhat hilarious suggestion was that we could try switching on all the Force's electric razors.

All this excitement didn't make for a peaceful night's sleep. By this stage of the war I didn't normally waste much time thinking about dying, but on this night I felt distinctly queasy. It was just over three years since I had had to swim off *Skipjack* and now it looked as if I might have to do a repeat. I was more afraid of being maimed than of being killed. Death in the water is quick but maiming is for life.

In the hot September nights I always slept on deck on a camp bed mattress near the radio offices and on this night I kept my blown up lifebelt under my pillow. I was taking no chances. I was up well before dawn in the radio office waiting for the warning signals.

A red hot sun rose out of a mirror-calm sea. The cloudless blue sky showed no hint of enemy aircraft. Then a distant very high radar trace was reported by one of the ships and the Red Air Raid Warning was sounded on the sirens, but our air patrols found nothing.

A few minutes later, without any warning, a massive explosion swept across the anchorage and I left the cipher office to see what had happened. A huge cloud of black smoke obliterated the next ship to us in our line, the British cruiser, HMS *Spartan*. The debris from the explosion rose hundreds of feet into the sky and as the cloud dissipated upwards we could see nothing but pieces of wreckage and a few survivors swimming in an oily sea. *Spartan* was no more – just a hulk on the seabed of Salerno Bay. *Biscayne* was the intended target but *Spartan* was larger than us and was probably an easier target for a radio-controlled bomb, which the aircraft pilot had to guide on to the target. Special Weapon X was a powerful guided missile and this attack was one of the earliest recorded.

Spartan suffered a terrible loss of life but she was the only guided missile casualty in the anchorage. Perhaps it was just a trial run by the Germans but such weapons were used extensively later on in the war.

In the American southern sector a crisis developed soon after we got there. The Germans had surrounded the assault force and prevented it from linking up with the British troops to the north. For a while there was some doubt whether or not the Americans could hold the beaches in their sector. If they had collapsed the position of the British force would have been dire and the whole landing might well have had to be abandoned as we had at Gallipoli. General Clark had moved ashore and set up the Army Headquarters, which now controlled both army sectors. He signalled to the Admiral 'make preparations for a possible evacuation of the Southern Sector'. The General was renowned for being a bit 'windy' and at this early stage of the operation the Admiral was still in overall command of the assault. The naval commander remained in command of all forces until the 'military are firmly established ashore'.

The situation ashore was serious and the Germans were furiously counterattacking but as soon as it became known that plans were being drawn up to take the troops off it would have had the effect of destroying their morale and they might have panicked. Admiral Connelly took the difficult decision to negate the evacuation proposal by General Clark. To my amazement he sent for me and told me what his intentions were.

He said, 'I have an important message for the General and I want you to take it to him at his shore headquarters. Explain to him there is no possibility of an evacuation.'

I thought, why pick on me, a limey, a junior Lieutenant RN? What had I done to deserve this unenviable task? Then I thought that if I have to do it I'll do it in style. I changed out of my dirty khaki assault uniform and put on my best white tropical kit. Only the RN wore white shorts and they did look rather cissy but were very comfortable in hot weather. Clad in white shorts, crisp white shirt, white stockings and white buckskin shoes I landed and walked up the beach feeling rather incongruous amidst the paraphernalia of an amphibious landing. The beach was backed by scrubby bushes and olive trees and rearing up amongst all the debris of the landing was the ruin of the beautiful Roman temple of Paestum. It was calm and impressive, a relic of an earlier civilisation, but I had no time to stand and stare at its beauty. I had to find the General's command caravan and deliver my message. As I walked nervously inland I passed infantrymen dug in in their 'foxholes', as if they were expecting an imminent attack. They were none too welcoming.

'Hey, where you going?' they shouted out as I passed them.

Challenged every few yards, I called out 'Personal message for the General from the Admiral' and marched on hoping for the best. I think the soldiers were so amazed at this white clad, limey naval officer, in his dinky white shorts and stockings that they let me through.

The caravan was in sight. In trepidation I knocked on the door, went in, saluted with excessive zeal, and announced 'Message for the General from the Admiral. He says that an evacuation is not possible'. I then handed over my envelope and nipped out of the caravan as fast as seemed decorous. No one spoke.

The next day the British Army Commander in Chief in the Mediterranean flew in to assess the situation and the battleship *Warspite* and further reinforcement bombardment ships were sent in to support the army. A bombarding battleship is an awesome sight. The shells from her mighty 15-inch guns sounded like an express train rumbling through the sky and she had a morale-boosting effect on the soldiers. Against strong German attacks the American soldiers held firm and gradually the battle surge turned our way and the crisis passed.

But not before another guided weapon attack, this time on the *Warspite*. I was on deck watching *Warspite* belching out shells from her big guns when she was suddenly and without warning hit by one or, possibly, two missiles. Quickly she began to heel over and I thought 'My god she's going to sink, like *Spartan*'. She looked very unstable but then she steadied and her list was brought under control but she was out of action and had to be towed back to Malta.

The Salerno landings had been fraught and we teetered on the brink of defeat. A defeat would have set the Mediterranean war back many months and Italy might have come back into the war.

Slowly the Allied armies battled their way to Naples but it took much longer than planned. Once the assault troops were well on their way inland my Ultra task was over. My next job was to be in charge of naval communications at Naples and the coast of Western Italy. So I said goodbye to the delightful Admiral Connelly and *Biscayne*. It had been a joy to serve him and my introduction into Ultra had been successful.

Living and working with the US Navy had been a great experience. I had learned a lot about the attitudes and lives of American sailors and had had the chance to work at the highest levels with the Commanders of an assault landing. Living on board had not been a lot of fun. Why should it be? But in the RN there was always time for a bit of humour and leg pulling. The USN appeared to be more bureaucratic than ours and junior officers had less scope for taking decisions and using their own initiative. Although in some ways their officer-rating relationships were more democratic than ours their punishments for minor misdemeanours seemed harsh to us. I wouldn't have missed the experience for anything.

Chapter Twelve

Exhilaration

Tin Opening

An American patrol boat came alongside and whisked me and my team of communicators off to Capri. We roared off at thirty knots, skimming through the azure waters of Salerno Bay towards the perpendicular shape of Capri, which looked rather like an elephant taking a bath. Why were we going to Capri? The German army had fought a skilful delaying action in the hills above Salerno and had held up our capture of Naples. Flag Officer, Western Italy, and his staff and the nucleus of the port opening party were holed up on Capri waiting for Naples to fall. The rest of the Port Party was struggling along in the rear of the army on the mainland.

After two hectic weeks in *Biscayne* I was on my way to my next job, Signal Officer to Flag Officer, Western Italy. I was to be responsible for port and sea communications in his command, which ran from Salerno Bay to any area to the north of Naples that had been liberated from the Germans. I had not been selected for this quite onerous appointment but the Lieutenant Commander slotted for the job had fallen by the wayside, ill or something. I was to have been his assistant. Now I found myself doing his job as well as being the assistant. I didn't get any more pay. But I wasn't in the least bit fazed by the prospect. How arrogant is the self assurance of youth (I was twenty-four).

Our recent work had been strenuous and our nerves were still a trifle touched up by the uncanny accuracy of the enemy's latest secret weapon, the radio-guided missile. It was a relief to stretch out in the sunshine and relax. Down our starboard side the rugged cliffs of the Sorrento peninsula soared above us and I marvelled at the villages of Amalfi and Sorrento clinging to the steep cliff side. Soon we were entering the harbour of Marina La Grande in Capri, formed by a breakwater embracing in a curving sweep a small part of Naples Bay. I stepped ashore on conquered soil, quite a thrill at the time.

I was now to have an extraordinary interval in my war story. There was nothing to do; my war appeared to have stopped and I was on holiday in Italy.

By this stage of the war, after four years of active operations, I had quite recovered from my earlier conscience-stricken concern about not being at sea fighting the foe. I was only too happy to enjoy a spot of lotus eating and vino drinking.

One of the joys of combined operations was the complete change from the rigidly disciplined life on board ship where every day runs to a strict and unchanging routine. You were left to your own devices and were expected to sort any problems by yourself. No transport? Well, requisition a local lorry company. Not enough food? Then find the nearest US Army storage dump. The US Army were usually more accommodating than the British Army and they had a better selection of menus.

We jumped ashore from our speedboat and were informed that the naval headquarters was a few hundred feet above us in the main town. There was no sign of any transport so we had lunch, sitting in the sun on the breakwater, a gourmet meal consisting of dried biscuits and spam and some warm water from our water flasks. After lunch I set about finding how to get my party and their kit bags up the steep incline to the town. A naval despatch rider appeared on his motorbike.

'Everyone's up in the town,' he told us. 'There's transport there.'

But first someone had to get up there to organise it. This was no time to fuss about my status and officer-like gravitas.

'If I hopped on the back of your bike could you take me up the hill?' I asked.

'Hop on…sir'.

The road wound up between stone walls, over the top of which I could see lush vineyards sprawling up and down the steep hillside. At the top of the hill we stopped opposite a magnificent villa, its wide open-faced front opening on to the Bay of Naples below. Inside, the rooms were furnished in modern style with severe off-white walls and coloured tiles on the floor. The main living room opened straight in to the front and back gardens at each end. I was not surprised when I was told the house belonged to Count Ciano, the Foreign Secretary in Mussolini's government and also his son in law.

Our Admiral had taken the place over intact with its retinue of servants and he was using it as his house and as the naval officers' mess. Rear Admiral Morse was a delightful, courteous man, highly intelligent and approachable. He greeted me on my arrival and arranged for some requisitioned transport to collect my sailors from the jetty. Across the road two more villas accommodated the combined party of some thirty naval ratings.

I was hot, dirty, thirsty and hungry. The top priority was to have a bath, followed by drinks on the terrace and a superb dinner served by immaculate waiters wearing white gloves. It was a far cry from the hot, sweaty life on board ship.

That night after dinner we sat on the terrace in a setting of such peacefulness that war seemed planets away from us, except for the lurid glow of burning Naples ten miles across the black sea reminding us of untold miseries on our doorstep. We were to grow used to that pyramid of flame as it rested there throughout our stay, reducing Vesuvius's red and flickering tongue into a pale comparison. That night I sank gratefully into my luxury bed between cool sheets after a fortnight of a hard mattress on a steel deck.

I had no work to do until Naples was captured so I became a tourist and boated into the famous Blue Grotto, climbed the far rocky hills, sipped wine in the busy little square and bought extravagant souvenirs. This lasted four days and then I was despatched to Ischia, which is an island on the other side of Naples bay. We were to collect any ex-enemy, i.e. Italian, radio and radar equipment for further use.

Ischia is an island three or four times the size of Capri and more fertile and beautiful, but it was only two and a half miles from the mainland still occupied by the Germans, who took exception to our using the little harbour as an advanced base for a commando unit. They shelled it occasionally as a mark of their displeasure. The island garrison consisted of some forty US paratroopers and one hundred Royal Marine commandos, who were often away all night leaving their visiting cards on the enemy's front doorstep. Still living on the island were two thousand Italian soldiers, lately our hated enemy and now pretending to be our brothers in arms. It seemed a trifle precarious.

The Italian Armistice had not only taken Italy out of the war but they had also changed sides and become what was termed a co-belligerent, a sort of second class ally. This had happened overnight. But we were never quite sure whether or not everyone knew the new rules.

My party and I left Capri in a fast patrol boat timed to arrive in the little harbour after dark. The day before the enemy had destroyed a fast patrol boat, like ours, entering the harbour, so arrivals and departures were kept to the dark hours. We entered in complete safety and nothing could have been more peaceful as we humped our kit bags on to the cobbled quayside of the town, silent in its curfew.

I had four men with me and I had been given the name of a good hotel. When we arrived I tried my few words of Italian greeting, '*Buon giorno*', and was struggling to explain our needs when the manageress replied in perfect English with a delightful Edinburgh accent. She was a Scotswoman married to an Italian. The hotel was beautifully situated amidst pine trees and gardens that straggled down to a sandy beach a hundred yards from my bedroom window through which I could hear the gentle murmur of the sea.

The only other guests were a few Allied officers: a US Army Captain who was acting as Civil Governor and two young British naval officers; one acting as the naval officer in charge of the port and the other as his assistant. The problems confronting this small team (none of them intended for these jobs) were amazingly widespread.

The young Naval Officer in Charge had the job of rounding up any remaining suspicious fascist military and disarming them whilst keeping the loyal (to us) Italian soldiers fed and, if possible, engaged in the war on our side. Most of them were employed in coastal artillery units and the Governor and the Naval Officer in Charge decided they should fire their pieces at the enemy just over two miles away on the mainland. This was agreed with the Italian Commanding Officer. Several shells winged on their way and landed in the sea about half way to the far shore. A few more salvoes were fired with much the same result. And that was the end of the great artillery barrage. Was it deliberate or was it just inefficiency? At this stage of the war in Italy it was a strange mix-up. Having two thousand unemployed ex-enemy soldiers around us was mildly disturbing.

More worrying for the Allied team was the lack of food. In normal times the island drew its supplies from Naples, still in German hands, and this was causing great hardship. The local population believed that anyone in Allied uniform, whatever his rank, was an authority who had at his disposal vast granaries and Aladdin's caves full of food. 'Pane, Pane', echoed in our ears wherever we went. We did what we could to eke out some military rations, but the wretched Ischians went through a hard time of empty bellies. The only ones who did well were the owners of lorries and cars because we took most of them over for military purposes and compensated them. I had a lorry allocated to me for the collection of the radio equipment from outlying stations.

Each morning about nine, after a glorious bathe in the bay and breakfast, I would set off for the day with my band of four and scour the countryside for radio gear. As our chugging lorry lumbered up the hills we could see mile upon mile of green terraces where the vines were growing right down to the sea. When we felt thirsty it was only a moment's business to jump out and select a few bunches of grapes and jolt on our way, munching and trying to catch passers-by with our pips. The air was like wine, the sun not too hot and the people embarrassingly friendly. These were perfect days ending in long hot baths and dinner in the hotel. After three such days I had raked in all the gear I needed so decided to cast my net further afield and look at Ventotene, a rocky island forty miles north of Ischia.

After some difficulty I managed to get a local schooner to take me and my men to the island. The sea was glass calm but it still took us about six hours to reach the island. As we drew alongside the jetty what looked like the whole population of seven thousand crowded to meet us and I soon discovered they thought I was an Allied official bringing bread.

'Pane, pane,' they shouted.

'Niente pane, niente pane,' I replied.

It was about as far as my Italian would go. Then a toothless ancient thrust himself forward

'I speaka da Engleesh. Me in New York many years.'

I thought it must have been a long time ago as his vocabulary was scanty. After many repetitions I got him to understand that I had no food on board the schooner and that I would bring their plight to the notice of the Allied authorities. I feared this distant little island would not be high on the priorities of AMGOT (the Allied Military Government of Occupied Territories).

On our way back we passed a barren rock island and on its crest was a massive prison building, which was believed to house Italian prisoners who had opposed the fascist government of *Signor* Mussolini. We had not yet formally captured these islands but I hoped they would soon be released.

Chugging back across a sea as smooth as marble with the Italian coastline just a mauve blur on the horizon it seemed a pity not to have a swim and cool off. 'Stop please,' I asked the skipper. He regarded me anxiously and it dawned on me that he might think we were going to take over his boat and ditch him over the side. So I made swimming motions and made as if to dive overboard. He got the message and we stripped off and dived in. Then, as I swam around with the rest of my team also in the water, it suddenly occurred to me that the skipper might be a closet fascist and he might steam away, leaving us to our fate. Here we were in the middle of the Mediterranean miles from the shore and no one would know. One by one we would drown. I have always suffered from an overheated imagination and we had a glorious bathe; there's nothing like swimming in the nude. Today I would first of all have to make a risk assessment of having a swim thirty miles offshore and get a security clearance for the skipper and his crew before diving over the side.

That was to be my last perfect day for months. The holiday was over and I returned to Capri next day en route for Naples at last. On the evening of 1 October 1943 a signal was received from Army Headquarters that Naples had fallen. Our Admiral, who had been waiting patiently on Capri for many days, decided to go over early next morning to survey the situation before moving the naval port party into the city. On Capri we only had a small part of the total port party. The rest of them had made their way by road following up behind the Army. In all, the party was several hundred strong, staff officers, radio operators, signalmen, despatch riders, carpenters and skilled men of many trades. Port opening was known as 'tin opening' in the combined ops trade because, until you opened the tin, you couldn't be sure what was inside and that proved very true of Naples.

The next morning the Admiral, his Chief of Staff and I embarked in the Crown Prince of Italy's ceremonial barge (the Crown Prince was in Rome still in enemy hands). The barge was a spoil of war. It was a fine sleek power boat capable of thirty knots furnished with a sumptuous saloon, complete with cocktail bar (empty). The barge was escorted across the bay by two British motor gunboats. It was a disappointing day for the Med, grey and overcast with threatening rain. As we approached the city we peered through our binoculars to see what damage had been done during the fighting. At first the tall buildings along the sea front looked undamaged but there was no sign of life in them. As we went alongside the steps of the Excelsior Hotel a few street urchins and down and outs gathered anxiously and silently around us. Everywhere else there was not a soul to be seen. The long straight streets were silent; the once crowded shops were mute and shuttered. No traffic crowded the streets. It was a dead city.

The main port party arrived by road soon after we landed and we became quite a crowd in ourselves and the sad little group of hangers on held out their hands – '*Pane, Pane*'. We had none. 'Cigarette, Cigarette.' A few tender-hearted gave out some fags. After a quick inspection of the sea front the Admiral chose his headquarters in the Maritime University's comparatively undamaged buildings and we moved in to the hall for a hurried meal of cold baked beans out of a tin. Revolting.

We still had to collect the men and stores that had been accumulated on Capri and I was sent back there to organise the transport of men, stores and equipment to Naples next day. We had been on Capri for nearly three weeks and there was a mass of stuff to shift and I had to find shipping to do the job.

I requisitioned the local Capri to Naples ferry steamer, of about 400 tonnes displacement, and three smaller fishing boats and the forty-odd naval ratings on the island loaded all the gear and we set off in convoy. Each ship had an Italian crew and I stationed myself on the bridge of the ferry alongside the captain to direct his course through the minefield and to see that the fishing boats followed faithfully astern. I didn't want an explosion. We steamed out of Marina La Grande at a full five knots and headed down the swept channel. The captain spoke no word of English and I had rudimentary Italian, but he got my meaning and we wound our way across the bay with our slow fishing boats chugging astern. The crossing took about three hours and I was relieved when we berthed safely off the promenade of the Excelsior Hotel, a stone's throw from the steps where Lord Nelson used to land to court his Lady Hamilton 150 years before.

A conquered city is a pitiful sight. Although the Italians were now on our side this important port had been in Fascist hands until a few days before our occupation and the Local Authorities had fled with the Germans. The streets were filled with rubble and domestic rubbish; dead horses blown up like barrage balloons festered and stank in the roads. There was a stench of death everywhere, beggars crying out for food and skeletal children with hands outstretched for any scraps. The Germans had booby trapped many public buildings, including the General Post Office, which had killed many Italians when it blew up without warning. The sewage, water supplies and electricity had been wrecked. This great city was a disaster area and it would be a race against time to rescue it before disease struck down the undernourished, particularly the children, who are the innocent casualties of war.

The naval port party was only one component of a much larger organisation in which the American Army Engineers played a prominent part. The objective of everyone in 'tin opening' was to get the port up and running and the ruined city on its feet as soon as possible. Both we and the Germans had had a go at destroying Naples. The first priority in tin opening is to get the basic utilities, electricity, sewage and running water going. The docks had been badly damaged by the retreating enemy who had blown up ships alongside the jetties so that ships couldn't dock there. The American engineers had a neat way of solving this by blowing up the ships again in such a way that the ships' sides became jetties. Naples port was soon open for traffic. For my team the first requirement was to set up a radio station to talk to London, Algiers and our own ships approaching Naples. The radio transmitters arrived on the backs of special lorries and were speedily installed up the hill above the city. In the Maritime University, where the Admiral's staff was to be located, we installed radio receivers and communication centres for the decoding and distribution of signals.

The Headquarters Ship HMS *Hilary* was brought into the docks to act as a temporary headquarters for the Admiral and his staff until we could get the University ready. By the time we had cleared the shattered glass from our offices, furniture installed, portable loos rigged, water tanks filled and stores unloaded the city had come back to life. The clearing up process lasted about fourteen days and then we all shifted ashore and had to face the rigours of accommodation in an ancient fort, Forte del Uovo, as *Hilary* was required elsewhere. Rising at 6.30 am to pick one's way down a glass strewn corridor to a wash place with very few basins, but plenty of cold water that didn't lather, was not a rollicking start to the day. Then down to breakfast in a windowless room to enjoy cold corned beef, biscuits, margarine and marmalade and what was known as compo tea (tea that is premixed with milk and some sugar and disgusting to taste). Not a good start to a long working day.

We were very busy in those first few weeks and my day started sharp at 7.45 am in a beautiful office, lately a university don's sanctum, looking straight on to Naples Bay just across the road and Capri and Vesuvius framed in the wide full length windows. During the first two months it was a rare occurrence to stop work before midnight. Then with infinite weariness I would sally forth into the Neapolitan night and be greeted with the glorious freshness of the sea while high up in a velvet sky Vesuvius vomited its uncanny orange flame. I enjoyed that short walk back to our quarters and a fall into bed, a hard canvas camp bed, and oblivion until 6.30 next morning. This was a big job, which I had unexpectedly inherited, and I was determined to make a success of it and sweated my guts out to prove I could do it.

A suite of lecture rooms was filled with radio receivers and code rooms and offices. I was well supported by a team of officers, most of them the same rank as myself, which called for tactful discipline. My lynchpin was a marvellous little Channel Islander, Commissioned Signal Boatswain Jackie Condon, small in stature but great in heart, who had earned his commission the hard way, starting as a Boy Signalman and going through the ranks. He supported me and even nursed me if we had a spot of bother. We became good friends and kept in touch until he died in Guernsey a few years ago.

I have no skill at electronics and I was most fortunate to have a young Commissioned Telegraphist who ran the technical side of the outfit. There was a team of cipher officers for the secret signals and a group of coder ratings for the encryption and decryption of the less secret signals. Radio operators manned the radio receivers, taking down coded signals from the Commander-in-Chief and the Admiralty in London and from ships at sea in our area and transmitting them from our Admiral to the same addressees. Signalmen typed and distributed the messages to all those in the headquarters who needed to see them. We worked what was called a 'Three Watch System', 08.00–12.00, 12.00–16.00, 16.00–20.00 and then the forenoon watch came on again from 20.00–24.00 and so on, round and round.

We couldn't live in the squalor of the fort any longer. Because of the booby traps left by the Germans the Admiral decided that, for our permanent accommodation, we should all be dispersed around the city to avoid casualties instead of setting up naval barracks and messes. Not more than six officers were to be accommodated in any one place. Four of us teamed up to scour the immediate neighbourhood because we needed to be near the University. There were many empty apartments because all the local fascists had fled with the Germans. One of our group searchers hit the jackpot, a luxury flat on the top floor of an apartment building. Everything was in place, including cook and maids who were only too pleased to serve us as they would be fed by the Navy and I suspect their extended families as well. Later on they told us the flat had belonged to the Mayor of Naples. We kept quiet about our find and enjoyed its comfort. Even in those plush surroundings it took some time before we had running water. Each of us returning from work would carry a container of water from the local bowser. The loos were the problem.

Although life in those early days was pretty miserable there was a wonderful sense of achievement in the port party as bit by bit normality was restored. The first flush of a lavatory after some barren days is a moment to be savoured, even celebrated. Fresh running water on tap must be the most desirable necessity in a civilised world. Slowly the city came back to life; the cafes opened; the streets were crowded and a babble of Neapolitan voices filled the air. When we had arrived local government had collapsed; the police had vanished; crime was rampant and the shops were looted. The miserable population of Naples had barely existed. By this stage of the war the Allies were skilled at 'tin opening' and could cope with this scenario and remarkably quickly had the city on its feet. Very soon the Naples Opera House was putting on performances.

Apart from the hard work and long hours there was little excitement in those early days until the German air force began nightly visits at around 7 pm. The raids were noisy and unpleasant and didn't achieve much except to scare us, as we had no shelter to go to. I used to sit like a stuffed dummy in my office trying to look British and getting on with my job as though it was only the neighbour's children playing a silly game. I never lasted a whole raid without leaving my work to walk round the radio rooms and communication centres where the men were working, simply to have their company though I tried to pretend to myself I was cheering them up. Apart from one near miss and a chunk of plaster that fell off my ceiling none of us suffered in any way from this nightly nastiness and after ten days it ceased altogether.

The front line was only sixteen miles north of Naples and the enemy was still putting up tough resistance along the line of the Volturno River where the Army had got stuck. I was given the chance to have a look at the forward area when I was asked to deliver some code books to the naval liaison officer attached to our 46th Division, which was operating on the seaward flank of the 5th Army. It was only about forty minutes' drive from the office and my driver and I set off at 17.00 hours. When we reached Divisional HQ they told us that the liaison officer had gone forward to Brigade HQ so we pressed on and after many wrong turnings discovered the HQ in a small farmhouse four miles from the river, but the officer wasn't there, having gone forward to contact a naval assault boat squadron that was preparing to cross the river. The squadron was part of the big push that the army was about to launch to capture the river crossings. I felt we were getting rather close to the front line. I have never been a keen land soldier so we drove slowly and gingerly forward as there were many obstructions in this forward area. We passed patrols moving up in single file to their assault points, tanks standing by and groups of infantrymen waiting for H hour, the hour to advance. It was fascinating to see these final preparations for the assault. It was an eerie atmosphere to see all this evidence of an imminent offensive, new to me, and to know that only two miles over the other side of the river the Germans were sitting and waiting too. Eventually we found our man close to the river and I was relieved to be able to turn round and put more distance between ourselves and the enemy.

We had only gone about four miles when we were startled by a long ribbon of flame ahead of us streaking across the night sky, followed by a shattering roar. I realised this was the opening salvo of our artillery barrage. It was a strange experience to be driving straight into this mighty roar and flash of lightning, which erupted every half minute, growing louder and louder as we got nearer, and to see the gun crews in the glare of the flashes as we passed through the firing zone. We travelled on towards Naples leaving the guns behind us until they were just a rumble in the background. Then we stopped and watched this magnificent spectacle.

The next excitement, of a different kind, was an illustrious visitor. The Admiral sent for me and told me that the Supreme Allied Commander, General Eisenhower, was paying us a visit and wanted to see the communications set-up. 'Keep it under your hat until it is announced.' Supreme Commanders don't often visit the serfs and I hoped they would be duly impressed and rise to the occasion. He arrived one evening when we were busy and I took him round the various stations. He showed great interest in everything and chatted away to the lads in a completely informal way. There was a magic about him, an aura. After he left we all felt seven foot high. It's a great gift when a Senior Officer can give such a lift to morale. After that I followed his progress to President of the USA with much interest. By the time Christmas came the work load had eased and everything was running smoothly. I was even able to take an occasional evening off and with an army friend we became welcome at an Italian home where the daughters made music and sang delightfully. I was beginning to enjoy Naples when I had a call from Algiers.

'Would you be prepared to go on another assault landing, planned for the end of January?'

I was far from sure but quickly realised it wasn't really a question more a demand. 'Yes,' I said very reluctantly. 'When will I be required?'

'Now and your relief will be with you in four day' time.'

Twenty-four hours to turn over and I was once more on my way to Algiers.

I left Naples with many regrets. After the hectic first weeks of setting up a complex communications organisation in Western Italy my team had shown they could cope with anything that was thrown at them. My own self confidence had grown and I knew that I could handle a big job successfully. My morale was high. Surely they couldn't do without me for the big D-Day in France. But they could.

On arrival in Algiers I was told that the next assault was to be at Anzio in three weeks' time and that my slot was a fighter direction ship, but I had no specific role. I was merely an observer and on the spot if any trouble shooting was needed. I was the Fleet Signal Officer's eyes and ears. This was entirely different from my two previous assault jobs where I had real work to do.

Anzio is a small port not far from Rome and it was hoped that we would be able to capture it quickly. The 5th Army was stuck fifty miles north of Naples and Anzio was well behind enemy lines so we hoped that a rapid advance inland from the coast to Rome would force the Germans to retreat and the Anzio forces and the 5th Army could join up for a swift advance north of Rome. The landing at the end of January was completely successful against light opposition. At dawn I looked out on a flat, grey coast and a small fishing harbour, which we rapidly captured. It didn't seem worthy of a major assault. Although it was my third landing it was always fascinating to see the hostile coastline, which I had held in my imagination during the planning phase. During the first twenty-four hours there was little opposition but we had a timid commander in the American General Lucas and he failed to press boldly on towards Rome before the Germans could rally the opposition. Lucas stalled and waited for reinforcements. The army got stuck 'like a stranded whale' as Churchill wrote. The German army reacted with their customary speed and soon the invading army had become the encircled army rather than the relieving army. Eventually in the spring the 5th Army advanced and raised the siege.

I was on board HMS *Boxer*, a specially equipped fighter direction ship, and because I had no specific responsibility I rather got in the way. Observers are always a bit suspect and are treated like spies. What's he for? He's reporting back to the Commander in Chief. I felt distinctly uncomfortable and bored. There were very few air attacks on the anchorage and none near us. After two weeks off the beaches I was recalled to Algiers. Did I achieve anything or contribute to the success of the operation? No. Did I gain useful experience? Yes. I learned how carrierborne aircraft were controlled and their strengths and limitations. It had given me a more rounded experience of amphibious operations but I was glad to be off to Algiers and a more robust appointment. Perhaps they would send me home for the big D-Day. Some hope.

Chapter Thirteen

Lotus Eating

Shore Job in Algiers

I was to join the Naval Commander in Chief's staff as a planning Fleet Signal Assistant, with special responsibility for combined operations. Apart from my signal course this was my first proper shore appointment. I was determined to enjoy myself and seldom did I have a twinge of conscience that I ought to be at sea. After nearly five years of hard grind and the odd bit of excitement I was ready for a more normal social life. The Wrens had arrived in Algiers and there was a bevy of beauties in the signal department. Normality had been restored and my mantra was that old cliché 'work hard and play hard'.

Algiers was a typically French city with native parts embedded in it. Set on a steep hillside, above a harbour enclosed by breakwaters, white villas were scattered up and down the slopes, with bustling streets below. The headquarters was in what had once been a fine hotel, but which had been sectioned into hundreds of box-like offices to accommodate the naval, army and air force staffs of General Eisenhower. The Hotel St Georges was high up in the hills and it had a commanding view of the harbour and the sea.

Reporting to the Supreme Commander was the Naval Commander in Chief, Mediterranean. Under the latter was his Chief of Staff and under him was the Fleet Signal Officer and under him was me. I was to help in the planning of the communications for the Mediterranean D-Day due to take place in June 1944 at the same time as the Normandy landings. I was also given the interesting task of planning the communications for the ports we expected to capture in France and Northern Italy, Marseilles, Toulon, Genoa, Trieste and Venice. I had always longed to see Venice, and expecting to be a Port Signal Officer again, I planned to become the Port Signal Officer for that city. I might as well get something out of all my hard work. I thought it would be a jolly spot to round off my war experience. Unfortunately, as Burns wrote, 'the best laid plans o' men and mice gang oft agley'. I finished the war in Trincomalee, Ceylon.

My boss, David Cox, appeared to be very laid back, which concealed a highly intelligent and sensitive inner person. He let me get on with my work without much interference but would always help if I got stuck.

Another person I saw every day was Harold Macmillan, the future British Prime Minister, whose title was Resident Minister with, I believe, cabinet rank. I met him on the stairs on my way up to my office when he was coming down. I say 'met him' but we never actually spoke and, in my ignorance, I thought he looked a rather dreary old man. If only he had said 'Good morning'. Why didn't I?

It was now the end of February 1944 and it would be a rush to get all the plans ready for the June D-Day. It was a seven-day week with long hours and occasional interludes of merriment in the evenings. We took all our meals in the aptly named Boozeria village school. Apt, because at suppertime, we were served the most lethal Algerian red wine and the future Lord Chief Justice of Scotland would regale us with a magnificent range of Scottish and bawdy songs. But we had to be in our offices by 8 am next day so we were early to bed. My bed was in a villa further up the hill as there were no barracks or officers' sleeping quarters. We each had to find our own accommodation.

I was billeted with a French–Algerian family, known locally as one of the *Pied-Noirs*. This description was somewhat similar to the designation of Anglo–Indian in India. They were French settlers who had at some time married a local African Algerian. They treated me kindly and I was very comfortable. I only slept there.

To get to my office I had a glorious twenty-minute walk in the sunshine in the cool of the day, down the hillside above fields and a valley strewn with wild flowers, and through the outer suburbs of Algiers to the hotel – a good start to a day of long office hours. Occasionally we had the evening off.

There were only two sorts of relaxation in Algiers, boozing or bathing. Swimming was much better than boozing. We had wonderful picnics on golden beaches on warm Mediterranean evenings. Even in wartime there are happier moments when the young can let their hair down and forget the war. Such for me was this six-month interlude in Algiers. I made a number of congenial friends amongst the staff officers: Bertie Grieve, who later became the Lord Chief Justice of Scotland; Teddy Souttar who became a priest but at this time was having an agonising relationship with a beautiful French girl; Charles Messer who became the Clerk to the Torquay Magistrates and Tam Galbraith who ended up as a junior minister in one of Macmillan's governments and fell from grace when he had a spot of bother with an Admiralty clerk. Quite a hotchpotch. I found a delightful girl friend in Rachel Somerville – lively, witty and beautiful, the daughter of the famous Admiral Somerville. The others were also well attended.

The eight of us used to drive (we had free use of a Jeep) out of Algiers to a quiet beach to disport ourselves, picnicking and dashing in and out of the sea. On one such evening, after a moonlight bathe, we went back to our picnic spot. No clothes, no towels, no money. Everything had been pinched by the local Arabs. Clad only in our bathers we had to drive back to Algiers. Algiers was policed by the American Military Police and they were humourless and unimaginative. As we reached the first check point we were stopped. 'Identity. ID pass?'. We had none and our foolish and semi-naked badinage cut no ice, as it might have with a British naval patrol. We eventually flannelled our way through by acting the typical toffee-nosed British officer type, which of course we were.

However, their disapproval was as nothing compared with the welcome the girls received on arrival at the Wren Quarters, where unfortunately the Head Bird was waiting to pounce as we were also late – absent without leave.

'A disgrace to the Wrens and to the Royal Navy. Officers are supposed to set an example. Get turned in. I'll see you in the morning.'

Luckily she had no jurisdiction over us men, but her look showed that she thought all men were despicable insects who should be squashed underfoot. We scuttled back to our Jeep and roared off. Next day I contacted Rachel to find out if they were going to have their leave stopped. No; the Head Bird must have been a better sport than we first thought. Apparently she lambasted them and said 'Don't let it happen again', which we didn't. Not that I had much chance as, sadly, I soon had to go back to sea to assault the French Riviera. Not nearly so much fun. *C'est la vie.* These interludes of picnicking and partying were actually far and few between because work took up most of our time.

Despite these happy times most evenings were spent working until supper time in the Boozeria School and afterwards the uphill walk to my 'digs' through the balmy Mediterranean night and another early start next day.

A blow was struck to our plans when many of our landing ships and craft were ordered home to boost the Normandy landings as the original plan was deemed to need reinforcing. Our landing in the South of France was downgraded and put off till August. This was a bitter disappointment and ruined any chance of our assault providing a pincer movement with the landings in the north. In fact, it was largely a waste of time and effort except that it provided the French colonial army the chance to fight. Up to now the French military effort had been subsidiary to the Allied campaigns. Our delayed D-Day was now 15 August, two months after our original planned D-Day.

This gave me time to check my plans carefully. Port planning requires close attention to details, not my strong point. I had to work out what channels of communication were required for that particular port. Then there was also the manning to be arranged – signal officers, cipher officers, radio operators, technicians and signalmen and the code books and many other publications that would be needed. It was fascinating work, rather like completing a jigsaw puzzle with, gradually, all the pieces fitting together.

Towards the end of my time in Algiers my young brother arrived in harbour. He had been called up at the age of eighteen and was now an Ordinary Seaman in the battleship HMS *Howe*. It was wonderful to see him again but meeting wasn't easy. He was the lowest of the low, not even an Able Seaman, and I was an officer. In those days in the Navy officers just didn't socialise with ratings from the lower deck, but I felt sure that in wartime the rules could be changed.

It still made going ashore together rather embarrassing, especially for him. After a bathe on one of the glorious beaches in which Algeria abounded we wanted some supper. The Yanks are much more rule bound than we are and their military police ruled Algiers. Every café and restaurant was labelled 'Officers Only' or 'Other Ranks Only'. We had to be in uniform so we were conspicuous. As we tried to get into a small café with the sign 'Officers Only' the police pounced. 'Can't you read *sir?*' That café is reserved for officers: other ranks are not permitted.' There was no use explaining that my friend was my brother and that he would behave in a most officer-like way at table. He wouldn't eat his peas off his knife. Not funny. 'On your way.'

We walked on. The next café was for other ranks only. I decided that I could slum it for one night and there were no police around. After the sunshine it was quite dark inside and I did not notice the black American military policeman lurking in the hall.

'Officers are not allowed in here, *sir.*' When American military police want to be beastly to officers they always greatly accentuate the *sir.* By now I was getting fed up and hungry. After all I was a Lieutenant, Royal Navy, and he was only a Corporal. I told him that some of my best friends were 'other ranks' and I didn't mind feeding with them. I could take my jacket off and no one would know I was an officer.

'No sir, *out.*' Once more we tried to get into an 'officers only' restaurant with the same result. We ended up eating bananas and whatever was the equivalent of a Cornish pasty sitting on the harbour wall.

Having learned my lesson the next time my brother had leave I borrowed a Jeep and collected my girlfriend and another Wren and we drove away from Algiers and the arms of the law and found a delightful estaminet in the hills behind the city. No one there queried an Ordinary Seaman, a Lieutenant RN and two WRNS officers having a merry evening. French omelette, followed by steaks and fruit and cheese and a fountain of wine. The war and military policemen were forgotten. We drove back through the forest with a fiery sun setting behind the pine trees and a warm glow within.

In and around Algiers the French authorities had painted on the sides of buildings in huge letters the slogan '*Un Seul But La Victoire*', Victory our Only Aim. So we decided to encourage the many Algerian cyclists pedalling home, weary after their Sunday outing, by chanting in a rising crescendo '*Un Seul But La Victoire*' as we passed them. Thus we felt we had done our bit towards bringing victory one step nearer.

All too soon the time came to say goodbye to the civilised shore life of girls and midnight bathing parties and head once more to the hot, sweaty cabins of a Headquarters Ship. I was off to sea and all the excitements of another landing, my fourth and perhaps the last of the European war.

Being on a top staff had been an intensely interesting experience, which was new to me. Although I was a long way down the pecking order I had had the chance to see how a large international staff operated. I believe one of Eisenhower's chief strengths was the way he led these disparate staffs. There was little bickering and dissension between services and between nationalities. We really did all pull together. He had let it be known that any snide aspersions or unjustified criticisms against another nationality or another service would be punished by the officer concerned being 'returned to store', i.e. sent packing with a black mark. We were a multi-coloured tapestry, American army, air force and navy and the same for the British plus a few French soldiers and British and American civil servants.

Years later when I was an Assistant Chief of Staff to the Commander in Chief, Northern European Command, in a similar international organisation, NATO, I valued this earlier experience.

Chapter Fourteen

Fulfilment

Operation *Dragoon*, August 1944

When I had come to the Med fifteen months before almost all my wartime expertise had been gained in minesweeping and I had a real fear of assault landings. I had read widely about World War I and knew that our soldiers and sailors had been mown down by machine-gun fire as they approached the beaches at Gallipoli in Turkey and I was filled with apprehension. Would I do or might I fail? Showing fear in war is always a poison nestling in one's innards ready to reveal one's weakness. Now that fear had been overcome. I had become an expert in planning assault communications and in installing a communications organisation in captured ports. I had been at three assault landings, each different but all of them intensely interesting.

I had become fascinated with the intricate planning for an operation. Communications were vital to success and a complex web of signal channels had to be organised to allow the assaulting forces to be controlled. The centre of the web was the Headquarters Ship with tentacles to all the commanders of the assault ships and craft. There was a galaxy of landing ships and craft to be woven into the web, large landing ships carrying the infantry assault craft, tank landing ships and smaller tank landing craft, landing craft carrying a bombardment gun or explosive rockets and bombarding cruisers and destroyers. This complex force had to be closely controlled and also be able to talk to one another. One of the strengths of the Med assaults was that the communications planners were also responsible for their execution on the operations. This kept their feet on the ground.

The work had been the most challenging I had ever encountered and I relished the pressure. I felt a sense of personal achievement and I was ready for anything. It might be said that I had become a trifle arrogant and this was to prove my undoing in the next assault.

I was still bitterly disappointed that I hadn't been sent home to take part in the Normandy landings. After three major assaults in the Med I felt I could have made a useful contribution to those landings and I longed to be at the 'big one'.

Dragoon had become an unnecessary operation and made little contribution to the winning of the war. The main German opposition was in the north and they only had light covering troops in the south. I suspect it was politically motivated by the need to give General de Gaulle some clout as it did allow the French Colonial Army a big part in this invasion whereas he had not been allowed to participate in the Normandy landings.

My appointment to the staff of Admiral Kent was similar to the one I had carried out in USS *Biscayne*. Now he was to lead the assault on the South of France at Fréjus in the Riviera in his flagship USS *Catoctin* – Operation *Dragoon*, D-Day 15 August. I was to provide him with an Ultra service as I had at Salerno for Admiral Connelly, but there was virtually no Ultra signal traffic and I did not get to know the Admiral or his Chief of Staff. In *Catoctin* I never felt part of the team whereas in *Biscayne* it had been entirely different as I knew Admiral Connelly valued my work and he showed it.

I also had a small team of radio operators and coders who would man communications channels to London and the naval Commander in Chief at Caserta in Italy where General Eisenhower had moved his headquarters.

As soon as the assault was over and Ultra no longer required I was to take up another appointment as Naval Signal Liaison Officer in Toulon, which would include setting up long-range communications channels in that port – more tin opening. I would also be responsible for the British signal stations along the Riviera coast from the Italian border to Marseilles – a pleasantly broad remit.

USS *Catoctin* was a purpose-built headquarters assault ship, splendidly equipped but domestically uncomfortable. Once more an invasion force was assembled in Bizerte Harbour in Tunisia. Although this was a familiar sight for me I still found it moving to look out over this mighty armada and there was always a frisson of excitement on the eve of departure of such a vast array of landing ships and landing craft, aircraft carriers, battleships, cruisers and destroyers and minesweepers, including sister ships of my first wartime ship, HMS *Skipjack*. Once again, next morning, I watched hundreds of ships and craft streaming out of harbour and joining up with convoys from the other North African ports.

The enemy had virtually surrendered the Mediterranean and we had a sunshine cruise across the sea, leaving Corsica to port, and anchored in St Raphael Bay before dawn. As the sun rose it lit up the beautiful St Raphael Bay with the seaside resort of Fréjus in front of us and the heights of the Alpes Maritimes towering over the far distance. Behind us the fashionable resort of St Tropez looked inviting. It was the most scenic of all the Mediterranean assaults.

Our immediate objective was the capture of Fréjus Plage and soon after the sun had risen the first wave of landing craft would hit the beach. I watched the sun rise in the bay and the sea was crawling with shipping. It was a perfect sunny day and it was going to be very hot. It looked like one glorious picnic. Little opposition was expected but as the first wave of landing craft roared towards the beach it was met by a hail of machine-gun fire. The long, flat sandy beach erupted in a ribbon of flame and smoke. This was too much for some landing craft and the leading wave turned tail as some tank landing ships had done at Salerno.

The Admiral was livid. He ordered his Chief of Staff to board the leading craft.

'Take 'em in: shoot any one who turns back.'

This time the soldiers were put ashore. The United States Army backed up by the French Colonial Army and British paratroopers further inland cleared the assault area very quickly.

In 1993 I visited the French Riviera again and found myself picnicking on the same beach. It was a bit different now: beach cafes along the front; families paddling and building sandcastles; a typical holiday scene. Then my mind flashed back nearly fifty years when I stood on the bridge of the assault flagship and watched the first assault waves of landing craft heading for the same beach at Fréjus under a blistering hot sky and being met by that storm of bullets.

The German effort was now concentrated in the north-west of France facing the British and American armies landed in Normandy. Our army headquarters moved ashore and the assault phase drew to a close. My Ultra role was over and the second part of my appointment loomed as Naval Signal Liaison Officer, Riviera. Why was 'Liaison' in the title? This was because of a complicated command set-up, mainly for political reasons. At this stage of the war General de Gaulle, the French leader, had become prickly about the lack of inclusion of French forces in the Normandy invasion plans. In Toulon there was to be a French Naval Officer in Charge, nominally in charge of the port, as well as a Senior British Naval Officer, assisted by an American Senior Naval Officer as most of the shipping was British or American. The port party was a hotchpotch of French, American and British teams all reporting to their national senior officers. It was a recipe for indecision and buck passing.

My remit was quite clear. We were responsible for the port's long-range and seaward communications and for setting up a communication centre (comcentre) to handle the signal traffic from those channels and to distribute the signals to all three Senior Officers.

I thought it was time for me to move on. I reported to my immediate boss, the US Navy Staff Communications Officer, and told him that I proposed landing next day to take up my next appointment. I thought he had agreed but this is where my inexperience and youthful impatience led me into deep manure and nearly a court martial. In the Royal Navy the word 'Propose' means 'I am suggesting that I do so and so' and, if your senior officer agrees, you can go ahead and do it. The tradition of the Royal Navy was to get into newly captured ports as quickly as possible so that vital communications could be rapidly established. A port without communications cannot operate effectively. At Augusta, Salerno and Naples we were in the port and setting up communications just behind the front line troops. I was determined to do the same in Toulon, the main naval port in the south of France. Drummed into us at Dartmouth and throughout our training was the mantra 'Always use your initiative. Don't wait to be told. Get on with it.' And that was what I intended to do but it does require a balance.

Chapter Fifteen

Pleasure

Tin Opening on the French Riviera

I left *Catoctin* with few regrets. The landing had been uneventful and the excitement of decoding important Ultra intelligence had been minimal, because there had been so few signals. My next job was to find out where the main port opening party was going to land and to arrange our route to Toulon. This was not the ideal way to enjoy the delights of the French Riviera, pre-war playground of the wealthy British, including my Canadian grandmother and her military boyfriend. It was 5 pm on 19 August, four days after the landings, and I was zipping across the St Raphael Bay in a fast motor boat with one signalman and one radio operator. We were dumped on the sands of St Raphael beach and had to find somewhere to camp for the night before meeting up with the rest of my communications team the next day. We found a ruined barn but far more importantly a standpipe with running water. By the time we had set up our little camp the sun was fading and the sky was turning mauve. There was no sound of battle and it was as peaceful as a morgue.

The next day I had to get to St Maxime to meet my main party on board their ship in the afternoon so we turned out at leisure. Unfortunately, the ship decided to anchor at the far end of the bay and there was no available transport. We would have to walk the fourteen miles from St Raphael to St Maxime with heavy packs on our backs. I decided to walk alone and leave the two ratings to be picked up later when we had transport. On my way I passed the Grand Hotel, damaged in the assault, and called in to offer words of good cheer to *Le Patron* and in the hope of refreshment out of the heat. *Le Patron* greeted me effusively in a darkened bar, sandbagged against bombs, and I was the only customer. 'Champagne, *Monsieur?*'

'*Merci, certainement, vive la France,*' I replied, hoping for a discount.

My conversational French was reasonable, particularly when gently lubricated. '*Vive les Allies,*' he toasted. '*Vive* Churchill; *Vive* de Gaulle; *à bas les Allemands.*' And so it went on until the bottle was empty. Then with a kiss on both cheeks I staggered forth to find St Maxime and my team. After a steamy walk and one welcome hitch I arrived just in time to greet them, somewhat effusively, as they landed.

The first problem had been solved: to find and assemble my port opening communications team ready to enter Toulon as soon as it was captured. Then we would rapidly establish the vital lines of communication to the Naval Commander in Chief in Italy and to the Admiral afloat in the assault area. The party consisted of two officers, sixteen ratings and two big lorries and trailers. But now we had to wait until Toulon had fallen before we could move in and sort out the communications. So we set up camp on the golf course, horror of horrors, but there was nowhere else to go. Just before we turned in for the night the BBC reported 'Toulon has fallen'. We only needed the military OK and we could get in there. Unfortunately, the report was untrue.

The next morning I went off to the flagship to confirm the BBC report and to discover what was being done to send the port party on to Toulon. On board a mental fog pervaded and I was told the Officer in Charge of the main port opening party had not even arrived in France. The only organised bodies in the area were the American and British port communications teams ashore. No one would give me any definite orders. It looked as if we were going to lose three or four valuable days in opening up our first French port, solely because the boss had not arrived. Here we were fifty-five miles away and no one seemed to be concerned. On my return ashore I discussed the situation with the American team's Communications Officer and he told me that he planned to wait for his senior officer. I said we intended to move up nearer and see if we could get into Toulon. I wanted to be the first of the port parties to enter the port.

On my return to our camp we started packing our gear into the lorries and we set forth with the White Ensign flying from the leading lorry with the crew perched on top of the equipment as we waved to the girls and old men by the roadside.

'*Vive l'Angleterre; vive le Libération,*' they shouted and we would gladly have liberated some of the young beauties.

'*Vive la France,*' we replied as we kissed them (not the old men). This war seemed quite enjoyable, but there was no time for stops. On to Toulon.

And so it went on through the pretty coastal villages with the crystal sea never far away. Suddenly we ran into a battle area, a dark stretch of countryside where the trees were stripped bare and shattered husks of houses in a village street tottered in the wind and an odious stench of death overpowered the sweet scents of summer. In the ditch lay a huddle of German corpses in the grotesque postures of rigor mortis, their skin as grey as their uniforms, just as they had been slain. A fierce battle had raged here. There was gunfire ahead.

A few yards down the road a French military policeman waved us back and ordered us to turn round. He warned us that a fierce fire fight was raging a mile down the road and to reinforce his warning there was an almighty crack from the fields on our right as the French artillery opened fire. Never a keen land warrior I ordered our transport to do an about turn and we hastened away from the battle. The triumphant entry into Toulon by Naval party 1068, led by Tony McCrum, had to beat an ignominious retreat. Obviously, Toulon had not fallen.

So we retired to the nearest town, Hyères. What to do now? I am not one for the rigours of camping, it is not really a naval pastime. After wandering round the town I saw the Hotel Mediterranee and decided to requisition it for my team. We were three officers and sixteen sailors. Being requisitioned was popular with the locals because we brought rations of food for their depleted stores and they were well paid eventually. Well, they had no other custom. The hotel seemed deserted but the front door was open and I went in. There was not a sign of anyone. Had they all fled? Eventually our heavy army boots reverberating down the long corridor disturbed an ancient manservant. '*Bon soir Messieurs.*' '*Bon soir,*' I replied. '*Dix-neuf chambres, s'il vous plait.*' He didn't bat an eyelid and soon had us installed in fine rooms looking over the Baie d'Hyères with a row of islands spread across the far horizon, the Isles d'Hyères. I was then led to meet *Le Patron* and *La Patronne*, a charming Swiss couple, and they gave me an enthusiastic welcome; they were pleased, they said, to be free of the Germans who had been billeted on them only a few days before.

'Did we want supper?'

'Yes, please,' and we handed over our field rations to see if the chef could make anything of them.

Throwing back the green shutters I stepped out on to the balcony and it was not difficult to forget those blackened twisted bodies and revel in the view of the wide open bay. Normally in HM ships officers live their separate social lives in the wardroom and the ratings live in separate messes. 'Never the twain shall meet.' Social interaction nil. By supper time it was hard to recognise the scrubbed and tidied persons from the grimy, crumpled khaki suits that had walked in a short time before and it seemed somewhat contrived in these luxurious surroundings to arrange separate feeding areas so I decided we could all pretend we were the high class guests who would normally be staying in such a hotel. We would eat and drink together. We sat down at one long table for our first cooked meal for some days. The chef turned our rations plus his veg into a gourmet meal and wine was provided by *Le Patron*. After the last of the plum pudding, which was part of our ration, the owner and his wife joined us, bringing a bottle of Johnny Haig's whisky, which he had stashed away waiting for the great day of liberation. Oh! What a Lovely War.

I suppose someone paid eventually. I signed numerous bits of paper and heard nothing more. In wartime it's fairly safe to sign pieces of paper. The reckoning seldom catches up with you.

Now *Le Patron* regaled us with stories of the occupation.

'Four and a half years ago when your ships left the bay I said the English will be back. Through all the days of the defeat, the Vichy Government and the German occupation I never doubted and now it has come true.'

Then, very solemnly, for drinking in France is a more serious business, we drank toasts to '*La Victoire, la France, l'Angleterre, les Allies.*' By this time some of our company began to wonder if we were enjoying a pleasant and strange dream. What an amazing world with the war so close that morning and now as far off as the moon. We enjoyed three days of such luxury, sitting in the sun, drinking in the evening and hearing horrible stories from the staff. I was busy every day driving back to St Maxime to collect the stragglers of our party and to find food dumps to replenish our diminishing stocks of action food rations. Eventually on 25 August divisional headquarters told us that the road to Toulon was probably clear but that the situation in the town was still obscure and great care was necessary.

I decided we would chance our arm and push off next morning to get nearer our goal. We organised a final supper party for our hosts and the staff who had treated us as if we were the wealthy patrons they were more used to. At 2 am we fell into bed and we managed to be on the road by 10 am. Amphibious operations tended to provide these bizarre periods when you wait for the army to clear the way ahead. Waiting for Naples to fall we had endured the luxuries of Capri and Ischia and now we could add Hyères to our list. Once we began operating we knew we would be working all hours of the day and night until everything was running smoothly. My team was in fine form and looking forward to new adventures.

Travelling along the coast road we saw neglected vineyards along both sides of the road and stretching away up to the grey-white hills which dominate Toulon. After our earlier experiences we kept a wary lookout for the enemy as we passed burnt out tanks, splintered houses and telephone wires drooped across the road. As we entered the suburbs there was no sign of any foe nor was there any indication of where our own authorities might be. It looked as if the fighting had been recent but the French military police told us it was all clear.

I decided to drive our party to the existing French Naval Headquarters as the most likely place to contact our main port party. This French Navy was the Vichy Navy under the Vichy Government, which had collaborated with the Germans, so I wasn't sure what reaction I would get. As the iron gates of the barracks clanged behind us and a small crowd of French naval officers and ratings surrounded us I had misgivings about our plan. These were the men whom we had fought in the past when we had bombarded Oran and Dakar after the fall of France in 1940. There was no cause for alarm; we were the first free sailors they had met and they could not do too much to help us. Being able to speak French to them helped a lot. They offered accommodation, which I declined. Instead, I asked for a patch of their parade ground where we could pitch our tents and park our lorries and trailers. Then I met the Admiral and his staff and explained that we were the advanced inter-Allied port party. I received a frigid handshake from the Admiral and he spoke not a word. He knew his hour was past. Two weeks later he was dismissed from the French Navy.

We selected a site for our radio transmitters and got busy to get them on air in the shortest possible time so that we would be ready to serve the main port party when they turned up. We had arrived safely with our stores intact and were all set to go. As we worked a racket of shelling and the sharp mutter of smaller weapons split the air around us. Had Toulon really fallen? Perhaps the Germans were counter attacking. I certainly didn't want to become a prisoner of war. All afternoon the work went on to the accompaniment of much comment from the watching French sailors, who asked endless questions about the war and our mission in Toulon. They appeared to bear us no grudge. They told us there were still some 10,000 German soldiers (probably an exaggeration) holding out in seven different fortresses around the city and that the place was by no means clear of the enemy. I didn't know whether they were trying to frighten us or whether it was true. Our own military had said the port was clear but to 'proceed with caution', whatever that meant.

By 18.00 the transmitters were ready to go on air and we began calling London and the headquarters of Supreme Allied Commander, Mediterranean in Italy and adjusting the tuning of the sets. Just before 10 pm London picked us up and told Italy that we were calling them. Soon after midnight the check with Italy was completed, and so to bed to the sound of the guns. We were ready to operate.

Next day there was little to do but wait for the rest of the main port party to arrive so that I could decide where the communications centre should be located. I would probably locate it somewhere in the dockyard so I decided to visit it and reconnoitre its facilities. Hardly had my driver and I passed through the dockyard gates than a most unpleasant racket arose ahead of us and behind us. We quickly ducked into a nearby air raid shelter where a French policeman warned us that the Germans still controlled much of the dockyard and reacted fiercely to any movement. As soon as we could we retired back to the naval barracks. Throughout the day the bombardment continued with intervals of complete silence and by evening pools of fire had sprung up around the city. From the barracks roof the city looked eerily beautiful in the clear night with its deserted havens shimmering under a dying moon. I still had no word from the main port party. What a shambles.

The next day, 27 August, there was still no sign of the rest of the party and I amused myself looking over the deserted German headquarters nearby. The enemy had shown a distressing lack of hospitality, leaving behind thousands of bottles of wine and beer, all empty. Life was beginning to get boring when the Senior British Naval Officer arrived on 28 August and told us the rest of the

Anglo–American port opening party port party would be arriving next day. Compared with the opening of Naples this operation was poorly coordinated and dilatory but I think this was due to the uncertainties of the command structure with French, British and Americans all involved. It was a complicated inter-Allied organisation with no very clear lines of command.

Now that the main party had begun to arrive we could start to organise our own domestic arrangements. It was important for the morale of my team that we should get an early pick of the best billets for officers and ratings as we had at Naples. We could not have been in a better position as we were the only complete party on site and I had had plenty of experience of 'tin opening'. We would have the best. All accommodation had to be officially requisitioned and the procedure was tortuous. One attends the Bureau de Requisition where one walks up several flights of stairs to find the official is not in; he very seldom is. Despairing of ever finding the right man the best bet is to find a friendly native and ask him to show you suitable hotels. They are mostly empty, locked and shuttered to avoid damage in the fighting, but the keys can usually be found with a willing neighbour. Then comes an inspection and, if satisfied, sentries are placed on the doors and previously prepared labels headed '*REQUISITIONEZ PAR LA MARINE BRITANNIQUE*' are stuck on all the doors. The place is then illegally yours.

When, eventually, one finds the *Chef de Requisition* he fills in the forms, directs you to other offices, all as far apart as possible, and tells you that you cannot move in until an inventory has been taken. As thirty-five sailors have already unpacked and established themselves in the hotel this is an illusion. After final visits to the office of the Mayor and the Sub-Prefect the legal niceties have been completed. Two hotels had been fixed up for my little band, one for the ratings and, across the road, another for the officers.

The officers and I were very comfortable in our hotel, which had an excellent chef and housekeeper. All seemed to be set fair except I had a most disturbed first night. Noises at the top of the hotel kept me awake and in the morning I sent for *Madame* the housekeeper to enquire the reason for all the shouting and banging. Very delicately she explained that I had taken over a well known hotel bordello – a high class brothel – and that she had retained the top floor for the 'trade'. Rather pompously I told her the Royal Navy did not share accommodation with such an establishment. 'Everybody out,' I said, 'and that includes you.' It was the first time I had slept in a brothel and I wasn't too keen on the story getting out. Of course the ratings thought it hilarious and suspected I knew exactly what I had requisitioned. If it had been their hotel I suspect they would have kept it in the dark.

After sorting the accommodation problems I decided we needed more transport for such a wide flung command, which stretched from Marseilles, thirty miles to the west, to the Italian border, ninety miles to the east. One of our maids told me she had worked for an Englishman who had had to flee the invasion in 1940 and who had hidden his Rolls-Royce in a shed. She knew where it was and took me to see it, a magnificent beast of chrome and lacquer, which even had petrol in it. I had never driven a Rolls-Royce and was sure that the owner would be delighted if the liberators needed to use it. It didn't matter much if he didn't. Thus throughout the Riviera I was able to drive in the style to which I was not accustomed, but greatly enjoyed.

There was much to be done in those early days and we all worked hard and long hours to become an efficient signal system serving all three Allies. I made many visits along the coast to see our coastal stations and this was where the Rolls came in useful.

Our equipment, 100 tons of it, had to be unloaded by hand due to the destruction in the port. Much of it had to be driven to Marseilles, our other large port. Earlier I had driven over there to do a recce for a local radio station site. No one had warned me that there were still some outlying points of German resistance. As I drove through the suburbs towards the docks I came across a couple of dead horses, hugely inflated, and no sign of life anywhere. It looked distinctly odd and I stopped the car. By now I was quite experienced in the atmosphere of a contested area and this looked very fishy. Officially it had been liberated but it had a front-line feeling. So I was not surprised to see a tank with large black crosses on it, a German Tiger tank, trundle across the T-junction ahead of me pursued by the French army. I turned round and beat it for home. I was never meant to be a soldier. It took a few more days to flush out the last of the German resistance.

After a few weeks the signals organisation was running smoothly and the next important business was to locate a football pitch. Volunteers soon found one near the railway station belonging to a local football club who were delighted to give us a game. As none of my team had taken any violent exercise for many weeks it wasn't really a fair contest, but it should be fun. I set out to watch them play. Little did I know what I had let myself in for. Standing on the touchline I was approached by the Captain of the French team who led me by the hand to the centre of the pitch where he presented me with a large bouquet of flowers and a kiss on both cheeks. The local band then played 'God Save the King' very slowly, followed by a rousing rendering of the Marseillaise. There is no instruction in the 'Seaman's Handbook' as to what one should do with a bunch of flowers during a national anthem. Should you present arms with them or place them reverently on the ground? The whistle blew and *le football* began. The Brits lost as usual but much bonhomie resulted and we were invited to use the ground whenever we wanted to.

After the hard grind of the first weeks I was feeling rather pleased with myself. We had comfortable quarters, roomy offices and well equipped communications centres. Our radio station up the hill was working perfectly and the troops seemed happy working a three watch system. Domestically they were well looked after as I had retained the hotel staff to do all the chores, which normally they would have had to do between their watches. All was well in our world.

The inter-Allied chain of command was so confused that I got on with my job unhindered by fussy senior officers. My real boss was the Fleet Signal Officer and he was hundreds of miles away in Italy. No one really knew what I got up to, a happy situation for a young naval officer. Then out of the blue fell a massive thunderbolt that I shall never forget. The Leading Telegraphist on watch presented me with a signal.

'Report forthwith to Admiral Kent on board USS *Catoctin* in St Raphael Bay.'

On my way to the ship I wondered what crimes I had committed. Junior officers are only summoned to the presence of the all-highest for terrible offences. I arrived on board; climbed up the long gangway; met at the top by the Staff Signal Officer, who said not a word; marched to the Admiral's cabin. There I was faced by the Admiral and his Chief of Staff who accused me of abandoning my post, disobedience and other lesser offences. No one asked me to defend myself and I was marched out. As I left the Admiral said 'I shall report you to your Commander in Chief'. I would probably get a court martial, disgrace and the end of a promising career. Why?

It was a classic case of the difference between two naval cultures. In the Royal Navy, even junior officers are encouraged to use their own initiative. Oral orders are enough to initiate action. The USN is more bureaucratic and junior officers are not encouraged to take action on their own initiative. I should have known better after my time in two USN ships. The real cause of the kerfuffle was a lack of clarity in my orders which read 'On the conclusion of the assault phase you are to establish port radio communications in Toulon as soon as it has been captured'. The Ultra signals had dried up and the army was miles inland and I had judged the assault phase was over. I had also made my intentions clear to the Staff Signal Officer and I thought he had understood and agreed but, apparently, I should have waited for written discharge orders. With hindsight I did act somewhat precipitously with the impatience of youth and a lack of judgement, but I had been trained in a 'tin opening' philosophy that encouraged the speediest possible opening of communications in newly captured ports. I drove back to Toulon under a black cloud to await my execution.

Some weeks later I was walking down the main street when a large car drew up alongside me. The window was wound down and Admiral Cunningham, the British Naval Commander in Chief, called out.

'McCrum, I hear you had a spot of bother with our American friends.'

There was a distinct twinkle in his eyes. The car moved on. *No execution: celebrations.* With that black cloud dispersed I could enjoy myself again.

Sometimes in the evening it was fun to sit in one of the little out-of-the-way cafes and talk French to the locals and eat delicious food instead of army rations. Somehow the French always manage to cook wonderful meals even when basic rations are short. At one of my favourite places *Le Patron* had a gift for story-telling and loved to tell us hair raising tales of life before *le libération*.

It was neither the Germans who were the villains of his stories, nor the British. His enemy was the American high-level bombers before D-Day strewing their missiles indiscriminately around Toulon. With much gesticulation he would extol '*Les bombes, par ici, par la, partout*' and with high drama '*Boum, boum, boum*' as he thumped the table to simulate the exploding bombs. Then, I suspect because I was British, he added '*La Royal Air Force, très précis, très exacte, on ze target*'.

But what story did he tell the Yanks?

I did try to talk to many French locals and my opposite numbers in the French port party and to understand their privations under the occupation. At that time there was no doubt that the majority of ordinary French men and women were genuinely grateful to us British and did their best to show their feelings. We had done many things to them that they did not understand and which they resented, such as the destruction of their fleet at Oran and Dakar and the invasion of the French colonies in Madagascar and Syria. But these were as nothing compared to our refusal to surrender in 1940, an act that they all realised made possible their eventual freedom. Today in Britain we tend to forget the prestige we won before the whole free world by standing alone against the Nazis.

Sadly the liberation of France was not the ecstatic event portrayed by the newspapers. Many French had supported the Germans, particularly the police who had helped to round up the Jews for transport to the concentration camps, and a paramilitary body called *les Milices*, who were active fascists who supported the German army and fought the French Resistance.

Soon after we arrived in Toulon I heard shooting in the hills above the city and I thought the Germans might be counter attacking. I asked some French friends if they knew what was going on. '*On tue les Milices*.' They are killing the paramilitaries. Anyone who had been a local member was put up against the wall in one of the old forts and shot. There was no mercy. The French called this and other less dramatic measures *l'Epuration*, the purification. They were trying to get rid of all traces of the Vichy regime that had supported the enemy. Who were we to criticise who had not suffered the indignities of occupation? But it wasn't pleasant, especially the way women were treated. Any who were suspected of 'collaborating' with the Germans were rounded up and their heads were shaven bare. Collaborating ranged from being a prostitute who had slept with the enemy to those who had formed normal close and loving relationships with German soldiers. One would see columns of miserable women being paraded through the streets between a mob of howling citizens. It was not edifying and there was much rough justice in those early days. I also suspect there were a lot of old scores being paid off.

As I talked to French friends, supporters of General de Gaulle and ex-Vichyites I realised that France was not at ease with herself. There was a bitter feeling in the country with factions pulling in different directions. Some were ashamed of their country and they did not seem big enough to forget their past and join once more in one titanic heave to put their country on its feet. That is why the French, suffering from a terrible inferiority complex, found the attitudes of the Americans grated on them. They disliked the brash way in which the Yanks showed their contempt for French methods and efficiency, yet they desperately needed the material and equipment the Americans were generously supplying. They had to swallow their pride and that only made matters worse.

Sometimes I was the middleman for grievances, from the French navy about the brusqueness of the Americans and from the Americans about French inefficiencies. Unfortunately, as I spoke French, and my American opposite number didn't, nor did my French opposite number speak American, I was commissioned by both sides to lay the various complaints before the appropriate authority.

In my team there was a radio operator, Jack Doyle. Why do I remember his name from amongst the many I have forgotten? Because…. After the first week in Toulon was over and work had subsided a little he asked to see me privately. He told me he wasn't Jack Doyle at all. He was really Jean Dubois.

After the fall of France in 1940 we had offered any French sailors stranded in England the option to fight on or return to France. If any of them feared reprisals against their families we would absorb them into the Royal Navy as British sailors, giving them a British identity and papers and a name of their choice. Our Jack must have had a neat sense of humour as he chose Jack as his first name (the name by which all sailors are known – Jack Tar) and the only surname he could think of was that of the famous boxer Doyle – Jack Doyle the heavyweight. By now, five years later, he had become the complete British sailor with all the vernacular of the lower deck and I certainly took him for one of ours. After explaining who he really was, he said, 'May I have a few days' leave to see my family'. He told me he had had no news of them since 1940 as he hadn't wanted to compromise them. They lived somewhere north of Marseilles. Of course I granted him leave and gave him transport to Marseilles.

A week later, not a minute late, he returned to work. His family was intact and he had had an ecstatic welcome. I then set arrangements in hand for him to be released from the Royal Navy and to become once again a French citizen. There were many like him and I don't think we ever fully repaid them for their sacrifice. Were they ever recognised? I would like to have met him again on his home ground. I have had a great affection for France and the French since my father took us to Brittany for two months in each of the summers of 1926 and 1927, when I was seven and eight years old.

In October the French authorities decided to stage a Liberation Parade. The American and British forces would lead the troops and the British Senior Officer asked me to provide the Colour Party as we had been in Toulon from the beginning. I chose our 'hostilities only' policeman, a fine six foot two inches of a man, to carry the White Ensign, supported by one signalman and one radio operator as escorts. They led the British contingent through the streets of Toulon to the cheers of the crowd, polite but not ecstatic. French sailors and soldiers, mostly colonial Zouaves (black soldiers from Africa) brought up the rear. As the French contingent passed the emotions of the crowd boiled over and the streets erupted in a barrage of cheering. At last the French could let themselves go. 'Bravo, bravo,' they shouted and many wept.

There was none of the social relaxation we had enjoyed at Algiers. There were no Wrens and no picnics and midnight bathes. By December 1944 I had been in France for four months. The Allied armies had broken out of the Normandy bridgehead and were streaming into France and Belgium. In the south the Germans were in full retreat. The war seemed to be drawing to a close. Some thought it would be over by Christmas. There was little left for me to do.

Since coming to the Mediterranean eighteen months before I had had excitements to last me all my life and responsibilities beyond my years. As a young twenty-four-year-old I had helped to plan the first invasion of the continent of Europe and had had an insider's view of naval high command, followed by a succession of fascinating and demanding jobs. I had had two rewarding encounters with the United States Navy, which were interesting rather than enjoyable. Although we spoke English and understood each other our respective naval traditions were different. The United States Navy has a marvellous 'can do' attitude, which I think is a special attribute of the American nation. They always consider any difficulty can be overcome and usually they achieve it.

I would not have missed my time in the Med for anything, particularly now I knew I was unscathed. It had given me a feeling of great self confidence. Through the Ultra system I had come into close contact with the Admirals and Generals commanding big assault landings and had taken part in the opening of three captured ports and had led the teams that got their communications up and running. It hadn't all been work. Girlfriends, fun on the beaches and for a short time comfortable shore living and new friendships. In my field of combined operations I felt supremely assured and knowledgeable. I was sure I could tackle anything. It never occurred to me I was still a very junior officer. This experience had given me the feeling that no future problem would be insuperable. Perhaps it was only youthful arrogance.

I was delighted in mid-December when a signal arrived.

'You will be relieved by X on 16th December and you are to proceed to UK for leave. Report to the Senior British Naval Officer, Marseilles to arrange passage home.'

At this stage of the war all travel home from the Med was by sea, via Gibraltar, and it took all of two weeks. The overland route through France had not yet been opened up. Christmas at sea in a troop ship was not my idea of fun. Then I had an idea. I had the Rolls. How would the wealthy British owner have gone home – by car of course, chauffeured by his man Jeeves. Although not wealthy I had my own Jeeves, Marine Daniels, my faithful Royal Marine driver.

My boss in Italy was unconventional and I thought it was worth a try on. If it succeeded I would almost certainly be home for Christmas. So I winged off a signal to my boss.

'Your signal, I propose to travel overland to Dieppe by service transport, which will be returned to Toulon by Royal Marine driver. Will inform Senior British Naval Officer, Marseilles.'

I didn't add that I would make sure my signal to the Senior British Naval Officer didn't reach him until after I left Toulon, nor did I think it necessary to explain what sort of service transport I had in mind. To my astonishment he replied 'Your signal Approved' and he didn't ask what transport I would be using. I blessed him.

Chapter Sixteen

Rapture and Despair

Christmas at Home

Final victory was in the air and we were off on a little jaunt unhindered by any authorities, free as the wind over the sea. We decided to drive through the night, taking it in turns at the wheel. There were no motorways in those days. Unfortunately about 4 am when I was driving I must have dozed off as the next thing I remembered was being almost upside down in a ditch. With great restraint Marine Daniels said nothing and with the help of some locals we managed to right the Rolls again and it went as sweetly as ever. We arrived in Paris late in the evening to find a battered but joyful city revelling in its liberation. We only had time to find somewhere to sleep and have a good meal. The next day we did the sights. The city looked drab but one could sense its beauty under the surface as sometimes you can see a lovely young face under the wrinkles of an old lady. We were up early next day and went on to Dieppe, where I said goodbye to Daniels and looked for a suitable ship to take me home

Decanted on to the jetty in Dieppe Harbour with my heavy kit bag I felt rather forlorn. I no longer belonged to anyone or anything and I needed to find some skipper willing to give me passage to UK. Dieppe was a base for our motor torpedo boats and motor launches and I hoped one of them might be going over to their rear base at Newhaven. Further along the jetty there was an anti-submarine launch and I went on board and found the Captain. Would she be going back to England? Yes she was and I was welcome. They were leaving the next morning and I could doss down for the night on the wardroom settee. We would be landing at Newhaven before midday. This meant I could catch the train to Portsmouth and change to the London and South Western line and be back in my Belstone home that evening. It would be 19 December and I was well in time for a home Christmas on Dartmoor.

There is nothing like a wartime homecoming and I had been away for over two years. England seemed like heaven. Belstone was another world, where the poor potato crop was the main topic of interest. Carol singing round the village, greeting old friends and gulps of sherry at each stop. My family reunited, stockings under the beds, turkey and plum pudding. As our family walked to church with the great hills of Dartmoor soaring up behind us war was hundreds of miles away. In our lovely little moorland church the service filled my heart with 'the peace which passeth all understanding' and as we sang 'Hark the herald angels sing' the church seemed to me to be filled with the angels themselves singing. Peace on earth was the hope of all mankind that Christmas 1944.

The war in Europe was nearly over. Although our armies had got bogged down west of the great Rhine River we were in complete command of the air and had far superior military forces. I looked forward to a peaceful and wonderful leave and a quiet seagoing appointment in home waters in the New Year.

I had been home for a week or so when a letter arrived from the Admiralty. 'Join HMS *Tartar* on 15th January for service in the Far East.' Although the war in Europe was nearly over the fight against Japan was still raging. After two years in foreign parts I had expected a job in UK waters. For the first time in five years of war my emotions overwhelmed me. I gazed out of the window at the desolate moorland scene and wept bitter tears. For five years I had become accustomed to daily dangers and hiding my fears. I had become happy-go-lucky, content to take each day as a bonus. The contrast with our peaceful home and village had pierced the fragile façade built up to protect me from the horrors of war. In a flash I felt a desperate longing for survival, to live and not to die.

I read the letter again … 'for service in the far East' … and the war with Japan, a brutal struggle, might go on for at least another two years. At that moment I didn't want to face danger any more and pretend to be brave. As I looked out on to the moor I longed to be able to walk the hills again in peace, to watch the clouds sliding across the valleys and to see the streams sparkling in the sunlight. My morale had crashed and my defences had crumbled. I had had enough. No more war. No more screwing up my courage to fight on. After five years I was war weary and wanted *out*. It was a total collapse, but as quickly as the spasm had hit me I recovered and controlled myself. I would go on to the bitter end and I must never give in. No one noticed my brief breakdown. It was all over in a minute.

Chapter Seventeen

The War Against Japan

HMS *Tartar*

It was back to destroyers, my third and also my favourite type of ship. They are fast and sleek, beautiful to watch creaming through the water at thirty knots or more. *Tartar* could do 40 mph. Destroyers brought out the best in people and. life in the wardroom was usually merry and informal.

By January 1945 the war was going our way. The Germans were back across the Rhine and the war in the west would end in the spring. Even the war against Japan had turned and after the enormous casualties they had inflicted on the Americans and ourselves they were on the defensive. The Americans were pursuing them across the Pacific from island to island and in Burma the Indian and British armies were recapturing that country. At sea the British Eastern Fleet, based in Ceylon, was also on the offensive at last.

After my leave my morale was restored and I was keen to get the war over and to enjoy my time in *Tartar*. Onwards to the end. It had been a long war, over five years so far, and it seemed never ending. Although the majority of the days at sea had been peaceful and without incident the dangers under the sea and in the sky above remained ever present perils. We were all longing for normality again and to be reunited with our families.

On 15 January I joined *Tartar* in the Hull fish docks on a cold, wet January day, such as is the speciality of the East Coast, but on board there was a warm welcome. The sun was 'over the yardarm' (there wasn't any) and all the wardroom officers were gathered for a pre-dinner drink. I was the outsider as most of them had served in the ship during its successful night operations in the Channel when they had sunk German warships. But they made me extremely welcome.

This was the beginning of a commission that turned out to be one of the happiest and most stimulating of my time in the Navy. We were a diverse crowd of regular and reserve officers, but with their war experience the reservists were every bit as capable as the rest. We all got on famously. Our Captain, Basil Jones, was a magnificent fighting destroyer captain who had been most successful in Channel anti-destroyer attacks, not an intellectual but a first class seaman and a joy to serve. He was also the Captain (D), D for destroyers, of the rest of our flotilla of five other *Tribal* class ships, each named after world wide tribes – *Ashanti, Nubian, Eskimo* and so on. This is why I was there, on Basil's staff as Staff Signal Officer, 8th Destroyer Flotilla. The second in command, No. 1, was Peter Ashmore who had lived next door to us when we were children and who later became an Admiral and then Master of the Queen's Household. A particular friend of mine was my opposite number as Flotilla Torpedo Officer, an Australian reservist, Sandy Nevile who had graduated at the London School of Economics and had similar left wing views to me. He was a delightful but volatile character who once hurled a full coffee pot at me in the wardroom because he thought I had been rude about Australia. I probably had but meant it in jest and didn't expect such a violent reaction. However, it missed me but made an awful mess of the wardroom carpet.

After the war Nevile reached the top in the Australian business world. We remained friends and he visited us regularly on his UK visits until he was killed in a car crash at the age of seventy-four – a sad ending. There were several other notable characters amongst the officers, our chief engineer who was nearly an alcoholic but managed to run a first class department and several comics who entertained us on guest nights. Both staff and ship's officers proved to be an excellent team. It was a most stimulating wardroom.

We were soon on our way to Plymouth for our work up as the ship had been in refit for several weeks being prepared for service in the tropics. The weapons systems and the communications all needed an overhaul and the new crew members had to be trained in their seamanship tasks. At this stage of the war we were getting many young eighteen-year-olds straight out of school and college and they were very green. Sailing back into Plymouth was a big thrill for me. My home country – but there was no time to go home. The entry into Plymouth Sound must be one of the most beautiful in England. The city stretches itself round all the little inlets and bays of the Sound and, as a backcloth, the hills of Dartmoor rear up behind it, looking quite high from sea level. Since I was seventeen I had been leaving and entering the Sound in peace and war many times, but it never ceased to thrill me.

Each day we went to sea and exercised with aircraft, submarines and sister ships until all our systems were fully efficient. The war at sea was still on but there was little danger in the Western Approaches, except from a possible submarine as the U-boats had moved in to coastal waters after their defeat in the Atlantic.

As soon as we were 'worked up' we set out for Gibraltar with other ships of our flotilla, only to refuel with no time to rekindle old memories of my midshipman's time. Then we went on to Malta, still much battered from the constant air raids in 1940–1943. Then through the Suez Canal and a baking hot Red Sea, with no air conditioning in those days. Then the long haul across the Indian Ocean with delicious cool sea breezes after Red Sea heat, exercising each day to improve our efficiency.

When we arrived in Colombo for a two day stopover I got a message from a very dear uncle, the only one I had, to come to have supper with him. He was a Rear Admiral ashore and in charge of all the shore naval establishments in Ceylon – quite a big cheese. His grand barge collected me amongst a certain amount of leg pulling about getting above my station. I thought I was going to have a quiet, informal meal with him alone, but he had laid on a dinner party for me. As the guests were incredibly ancient, all in their fifties, I didn't think it would be much of a wow for me. However, it was a relief to enjoy the luxury and cool of Admiralty House, a grand colonial domain. Uncle had always been a great party giver, kind and high spirited, particularly when he was well out of sight of his wife, my Aunt Cicely, who in her own way was a super person but much more proper.

Despite my misgivings it was a splendid party. The guests behaved as if they were young midshipmen and I was the one who felt a bit old. In those days dinner ended with many toasts; first of all 'The King' then, depending on the day of the week, the toasts of the day, 'Sweethearts and wives', 'Our ships at sea', 'Absent friends' and on Wednesdays we drank 'To ourselves' as well as any other toast one of the guests might suggest. By the end of the toasts we were all happily lubricated.

Then my uncle surprised me. 'Time for egg laying', he announced. The guests seemed unsurprised so I tried to look unconcerned. The Goan steward produced an egg, clearly expecting this extraordinary event. Uncle explained the rules.

Each of you has to pass the egg from your port glass to you neighbour's without it being broken and so on right round the table. If you fail you have to pay a forfeit, decided by the rest of the guests.

How on earth was it to be done? The steward placed the egg in the principal guest's glass and the trick was to blow hard down into the glass and under the egg and lo the egg began to lift and as it wobbled near the top of the glass an extra hard puff propelled it into your neighbour's glass. If the egg missed the glass you had to perform some ridiculous act or sing a song. Luckily there were plenty of eggs in Ceylon but I kept thinking of my family at home existing on one egg a month. After dreading a starchy old man's dinner I had a great time and was soon being wafted back to the ship in Flag Officer Ceylon's barge.

Our final stop was Trincomalee on the north east coast. As we steamed into the harbour, leading our flotilla of destroyers, we saw it was filled with our mighty Eastern Fleet. I hadn't seen so many ships since our days in Scapa Flow in 1940. There were rows of battleships, aircraft carriers and cruisers with another flotilla of destroyers tucked away at the far end of the bay. It was a majestic sight. The harbour was like a large inland sea, surrounded by low lying hills clothed in palm trees with the offices and stores of the naval base scattered amongst them.

The biggest problem the fleet had to face was that the Japanese fleet was a long way away, based in Singapore. To attack Japanese bases we had to cross most of the Bay of Bengal before we could fly off the Fleet Air Arm aircraft to bomb the airfields on Sumatra. It was nearly one thousand miles to steam before we could fly off our aircraft. This was our major task in early 1945 as we were preparing for the invasion of Malaya in the autumn in an amphibious operation codenamed *Zipper*, when we would land an army near Port Dickson on the south-west coast of Malaya.

The forays into the Bay of Bengal were almost entirely uneventful for the destroyers. There were no air attacks other than the occasional recce aircraft several miles away. Our job was to screen the big ships and protect them from possible submarine attack. The only real danger was within the force when we were zigzagging to confuse submarines. The carriers and battleships carried out one set of zigzags and the destroyer screen another one. This always called for extreme care by the officers of the watch to follow precisely the correct zigzag diagrams. There had been previous casualties due to human error. A cruiser, the *Curacoa*, had been cut in half by the *Queen Mary* in the Atlantic with the loss of most of her crew, due to human error. One of my Drake term mates went down in her. Apart from that, sailing into the Bay of Bengal was rather enjoyable, particularly on the tropical night watches in the evening's cool and under a moon the dark seas shimmered like quick silver and dolphins raced the ship. Zigzagging tended to confuse them.

The darkened shapes of the battleships and carriers astern looked like monster elephants and we had to make sure we kept out of their way. On a night watch on the bridge there was total silence except when one of the two lookouts sighted something to report and the only other person on the bridge was the signalman of the watch. It gave one time to ponder the strange ways of human nature: only a few weeks before I had dreaded facing the Japanese war and now I was ready for more and enjoying myself.

I had a talented team of signalmen, radio operators and coders, mostly men who had been called up for the war, but by now hardened and skilful communicators. They were led by two brilliant, regular Navy Chief Petty Officers who kept a tight hold on discipline. The communications branch often got the pick of the bunch when the eighteen-year-olds were called up and our lot were a diverse bunch from the top public schools to the cockneys from London's East End. I had many interesting conversations with them during more relaxed times in the night watches. Most of the young were politically left wing and demanding a new world after the war, which chimed with my own views.

We spent many days at sea sailing to a position where we were close enough to fly off our aircraft to hit the enemy airfields in Sumatra, principally at Sabang on the northern point of that island. For the rest of the fleet there was hardly any action and the only casualties were the aircrew who were shot down by the Japanese fighters and did not return.

There was one exception when a signal was received, whether from submarine reconnaissance or Ultra intelligence I am not sure, that one of the Japanese heavy cruisers escorted by destroyers was steaming north in the Malacca Straits between Malaya and Sumatra. The Eastern Fleet was sailed at full speed to intercept this force if it came out into the Bay of Bengal. In due course the Japanese were sighted by our reconnaissance aircraft heading west, then they turned about and headed for home. The Commander in Chief gave the fast destroyers the order to 'Chase'. This signal meant that each flotilla was to break off from its screening stations and steam as fast as it could to engage the enemy before they could retire into safe waters. The *Tribal* flotilla consisted of pre-war ships and were not as speedy as the other flotilla, a more recent breed. The R class flotilla soon left us behind, struggling to keep up our thirty knots. They found the Japanese force, now a sole cruiser, the destroyers having fled back to Singapore. The Captain (D) of the R boats, Captain Pound, son of the then First Sea Lord, directed a brilliant torpedo attack on the cruiser and sank her. They managed the difficult manoeuvre of surrounding the enemy in a star attack so that whichever way she turned there was a destroyer lying in wait, ready to pounce. It was a classic. We were disappointed to play no part in the attack and the fleet returned to harbour. That was the last action of the war in the eastern seas.

In between these expeditions into the Bay of Bengal we had brief sojourns in harbour when we made merry and enjoyed ourselves on the magnificent sandy beaches of Elephant Bay. It was so hot in the enclosed waters of the harbour that we worked a routine known as tropical routine, starting at 6 am and ending at 12.30 hours, because the afternoons were too hot. In the cool of the evening we could complete any work left unfinished. The custom was to enjoy a few long drinks before lunch, go ashore, lie on the beach in a pleasantly boozy state and dash in and out of the waves. We invented all sort of sea games, water leap frog, and tilting as in mediaeval tourneys, one person on the back of another versus a similar couple. The 'horseman' who succeeded in pulling his opposite number into the sea was the winner and eventually a champion emerged. So the months went by, long boring days at sea with no action, interspersed by a few boozy days in harbour. Heat was the main enemy in harbour. My cabin was immediately below the steel deck of the quarterdeck at the rear of the ship and it was just like being in an oven, baking like a loaf of bread. Even at night I slept naked with just a towel across my midriff to mop up the sweat.

The war seemed a long way off and by now we were all too hardened to worry about what lay ahead. We knew that in the autumn we were expecting to invade

Malaya on the way to recapture Singapore. The British and Indian armies in Burma were beating the Japanese back on land and were advancing on Rangoon, the capital. Our landing at Port Dickson, 280 miles north of Singapore, would have been a tough assignment as the Japanese would fight to the last man. Later on when I saw the assault beaches from the ship as we sailed to Singapore they looked most unsuitable, with large areas of soft mud flats, which would have been difficult for the heavy vehicles, even with steel mesh roadways. Our job would have been to bombard roads and dumps to prevent enemy reinforcements reaching the beachhead. I was relieved we didn't have to do the operation. It might have been a shambles and post-war accounts of the coastline and beaches appear to confirm this.

A welcome distraction from the naval routines was the General Election in June. Churchill was expected to win but there was a Labour landslide, which gave Clement Attlee, the Leader of the Labour Party, the premiership. Our dear Captain came into the wardroom for a drink, apoplectic with rage, his florid face as red as the rising sun. The great Churchill, the man who had saved his country, had been betrayed. Who could possibly *not* have voted for him. A stony silence all round the wardroom, then one brave reserve officer said, very quietly, 'I did, sir'. Then one by one the rest of us declared our treachery. We had all voted Labour. 'Good God,' he said and ordered another round.

My generation had grown up under the shadow of the Great War, 1914–1918, and of the stories of greedy profiteers making their fortunes out of the horrors of that war. We had grown up in a time of massive unemployment, dole queues and the Jarrow marchers. Our generation was idealistic and disillusioned with capitalism. Some of us thought socialism might produce a fairer society and we thought we should give it a try. We really did want a quiet revolution and a bonfire of our class ridden customs, hence the unexpected Labour landslide. I believe the majority of service men and women voted for the Labour Party.

A few weeks later in early August the Americans dropped their first atom bomb on Hiroshima and a few days later another one on Nagasaki with devastating results. Some 110,000 civilians were incinerated in Hiroshima and these raids effectively brought the war to an end.

With hindsight many have become critical of the decision to drop atom bombs on Japanese cities, but they hadn't been fighting for six bitter years, longing for an end to the slaughter, longing for a normal life. At the time I believe every fighting man and woman was delighted and relieved that the immensely costly landing in Japan was no longer necessary. In such a landing in the Japanese homeland many civilians would have died as well as thousands of Allied and Japanese soldiers and sailors and airmen. The total casualties would have been far higher than those who died in the two atom bomb raids. The assault on Japan would have made the Normandy landings seem like a picnic as the Japanese army would have died to a man defending their homeland.

Whatever history may pronounce on these raids they certainly shortened the war by many months, even years.

On 14 August the tinny little voice of the Japanese Emperor was heard ordering all his forces to lay down their arms and surrender to the nearest Allied command. At midday on 15 August the war came to an end after nearly six years, which was two years longer than the Great War of 1914–1918. We are so accustomed to the horrendous numbers of soldiers slaughtered on the Western Front in World War I that most of us do not appreciate that the numbers killed in World War II far exceeded those of World War I, as so many millions of civilians were indiscriminately slaughtered by the Nazis in Soviet Russia.

The total number of military deaths on both sides in World War II was 14.3 million, which included 264,443 British servicemen, compared with just over 8 million in World War I. Add to these figures the 27 million civilians killed in World War II and the destruction of lives in World War II is almost unbelievable. The world had gone mad.

On 15 August the fleet was steaming across the Bay of Bengal to attack Japanese positions in Sumatra and Malaya and *Tartar* was screening ahead of the aircraft carriers and battleships. It was as peaceful as a nunnery. I was the Officer of the Watch on the bridge keeping the middle watch (midnight to 4 am) when the news broke that the Japanese had surrendered. There were only four of us on the bridge, two lookouts, the signalman and me. It was a perfect tropical night, the sea lightly ruffled by a gentle breeze, stars bright in a velvet sky and a large moon throwing down its beams across the sea, which looked as if diamonds had been scattered over its surface. Only the darkened ships astern of us cast shadows onto this carpet of light. It was a night of magic. Up the voicepipe the wireless office called.

'The Emperor of Japan has just announced that all Japanese forces are to surrender to the nearest Allied Commander at noon today.'

It was a thunderbolt. Suddenly the war was over. No more fighting; no more death; no more fear or fear of showing fear. We could live normal lives, marry, and raise families without worry. It was unbelievable. Peace at last. When you have spent the six best years of your life frequently in danger and constantly concealing the fear the relief that it is all over is indescribable. I could have danced on moonbeams that night. I was twenty when the war broke out and now I was twenty-six and a feeling of ecstasy flooded over me

I was glad that the news had come through during the solitude of the night watch when those feelings of gratitude and ecstasy that swept over me were in tune with the beauties of the heavens and the sea. It was a sublime moment and I recalled those wonderful lines of Siegfried Sassoon's when he heard that World War I had ended and they perfectly mirrored my feelings on that perfect night.

Everyone Sang

Everyone suddenly burst out singing;
And I was filled with such delight
As prisoned birds must find in freedom
Winging wildly across the white
Orchards and dark green fields; on-on and out
Of sight.
Everyone's voice was suddenly lifted;
And beauty came like the setting sun,
My heart was shaken with tears; and horror
Drifted away. O but Everyone
was a bird and the song was wordless; the singing will never be done.

But there was no song for many of my friends from Dartmouth and *Skipjack* who lay deep down beneath the dark waters.

The operation was abandoned and the fleet returned to harbour to celebrate. Led by *Tartar* (I don't know why) the ships flew the flags of the victorious Allies – American, Russian, Chinese, Dutch, French and, of course, the Union Jack. From all the mastheads of the fleet the word *victory* was spelt out in gaily coloured signal flags. By midday the Eastern Fleet lay at anchor in Trincomalee Harbour.

'Splice the main brace' was ordered by the Commander in Chief. This signal orders a double whack of rum for the sailors. The origin of this order was that it was given in sailing ship days when the crew had completed the arduous work of splicing the wires of the main brace, a particularly tough task. Now it was only given on special occasions such as a coronation. It was also the only time that officers were allowed to drink pusser's (navy) rum. Sailors had a free ration every day but officers were not allowed a rum ration as there had been a lot of corruption over the rum in Victorian times. Pusser's rum is none of your Caribbean holiday stuff and it packs a hefty punch.

In the wardroom our Petty Officer Steward concocted an exotic and potent punch of rum and other elixirs. At six sharp, the sun well over the yardarm, we started drinking and toasting to 'Victory'.

After a few starters we remembered we had been invited to a full dress cocktail party in HMS *Eskimo*, a sister ship. Full dress hardly seemed appropriate on such a day and we decided to ditch the protocol as this would be an unrepeatable day in our lives. To hell with formality. We each climbed into fancy dress and felt much more relaxed. Bing Crosby, our gunner, not the singer, transformed his six foot four inch carcass into a Hawaiian dancing maiden with a long skirt made of rope's ends, a cute little bodice made out of the sacred White Ensign and a straw hat and the rest of us produced a weird and wonderful variety of costumes. We rowed across to the party as if we were South Sea Islanders, using paddles not oars, much to the delight of the Ship's Company who fully entered into the spirit of the day by pelting us with rotten potatoes as we paddled away from the ship's side midst cheers, jeers and caustic comments.

But how would we be received by our hosts all got up in their finery? When we arrived alongside *Eskimo* we found a most orderly full dress show in full swing on their quarterdeck, lit with coloured lights and gleaming with glass jugs filled with enticing liquors. For a moment we were taken aback by this scene of gracious formality but as we came up the gangway we agreed we would all give the ship an oriental greeting by swiftly kneeling on our knees and kissing the quarterdeck and offering a 'salaam' with both hands to the forehead. That broke the ice and soon everyone else began changing into fancy dress and all rank was thrown aside. The entire party decided to meet ashore later and continue the celebrations at the naval club.

Returning to our ship we found chaos. No one gave a toss for rank or seniority. The sailors were singing in groups and firing off rockets and flares and the coloured Very lights. On the bridge my signalmen were flashing their large signal lights like searchlights on to nearby ships and shooting off their quota of signal rockets. Every ship in the harbour was flashing Vs for victory and tootling merrily on their sirens. The searchlights of the fleet stabbed the night sky in a chaotic dance. What a perfect night, thick with brilliant stars, the tropical sky crossed by the coloured trails of the rockets and drifting star shells. Star shells illuminate a large patch of sea and come drifting slowly down and fizzle out as they hit the water but the shell casings can make a nasty dent in the deck or one's head. Not wanting to be left out of the fun I climbed up to the bridge and for the only time in my life I let off the big rockets and fired Very lights to my heart's content. Looking back it all seems extraordinarily childish but it was fun.

It had become one glorious, uncontrolled, anarchic party, but it was becoming dangerous. The flagship desperately signalled 'Cease Firing' over and over again but no one took a blind bit of notice. I doubt if there was a signalman capable of reading the signal. Nobody cared a toss. Stuff the Admiral. Eventually exhaustion set in and calm prevailed.

Meanwhile, the officers had changed out of fancy dress and were ready to go ashore for the next instalment of victory celebrations. Another tot before embarking in a rather unsteady motor boat (the boat or us) and then we were off to the club to 'beat it up'. By now there were about thirty of us from the ships of our flotilla and we danced up the sandy main road doing the 'Palais Glide', effectively stopping all traffic. There wasn't much. Arriving at the club we found rather a stuffy atmosphere with diners behaving as if it was a wet Sunday in Plymouth instead of celebrating a great victory. We decided everyone must enjoy themselves even if they didn't want to. We must have been pests. To get things off to a rollicking start we gathered outside the dining room and sang them some Christmas carols. Then we seated ourselves at several long tables and rained bread pellets at anyone we didn't like the look of. This sparked a bread war and at last the rest entered into the spirit of the night.

After dinner we started the traditional naval game where each set of officers shouts out the name of their ship letter by letter – T.A.R.T.A.R. – and at the end everyone shouts the full name. This is immediately challenged by another ship who try to out shout them. By this time the rest of the club's clientele had livened up and joined in the fun and the evening ended in 'Stair Racing', a fascinating game, ruinous to the bum. Two competitors sit at the top of a wide staircase, side by side, legs stiffly outstretched before them. A gentle shove and away they go down to the bottom, bumping from step to step. The winner is then challenged by the next contestant and so on until finally a stair champion is declared. It pays not to be the champion. Sore bums are guaranteed next day but it's hilarious for the onlookers.

Having celebrated VJ Day we were ordered to Penang off the west coast of Malaya, where the Commander in Chief was to receive the surrender of all Japanese naval forces west of Singapore. We anchored close to HMS *Nelson*, a 16-inch gun battleship, flagship of the Eastern Fleet, so that we could watch the ceremony. The envoys were expected to arrive at 2 pm but there was no sign of them until nearly 3 pm, when one of our destroyers signalled that she had sighted a small unarmed Japanese warship flying the white flag of surrender. She then led the surrender vessel towards *Nelson*. There was a strong wind blowing and the Japanese ship signalled that it was too rough to go alongside *Nelson*, but the escorting destroyer got behind her and chased her towards *Nelson* and finally she made it. *Nelson*'s quarterdeck was crowded with spectators in white tropical uniform, which matched the large white flag of surrender flown by the Japanese ship. We watched as the two naval envoys came over the side and saluted first the White Ensign at the stern and then the Captain of *Nelson* who received their salutes in total silence.

I watched from our bridge as we saw the two little yellow men bowing slightly from the waist and then they were led away to the Admiral in his cabin below, followed all the time by an armed officer with a pistol. After signing the surrender documents they re-embarked and sailed back to Penang Harbour. This set the seal on the end of the naval war in the East Indies and Indian Ocean.

The fleet then sailed down the Malacca Straits, which separate Malaya from Sumatra, to Singapore where we had been so ignominiously kicked out three years before. Each destroyer went alongside the jetties in the commercial harbour with orders to offer an 'open ship' to all our ex-prisoners of war from the notorious local Japanese camp at Changi. It was in this camp that the Commandant ordered the Bishop of Singapore to cease praying and when he refused he had both the Bishop's knees broken so that he could not kneel, but despite the pain he continued praying on his knees as best he could. He was an inspiring example to all the prisoners in Changi by affirming his faith despite constant humiliation. Changi had been a particularly brutal camp where many had been tortured and some had been beheaded.

We prepared a great welcome for the prisoners and food and drink in every mess was ready for a right royal party. We had completely misjudged the situation. The condition of the ex-prisoners was so deplorable they couldn't face normal food and alcoholic drink was unthinkable. They were still so weak that all they wanted to do was sit in a comfortable chair and talk, especially to ask questions, as they had been completely cut off from the world since they were captured in 1942. In most cases they had not received a single letter from their families in all that time. I had never seen such a pathetic and emaciated group of people. Each day different groups came on board and we went through the same question and answer session. Very quickly medical teams arrived and lengthy regimes were started to improve their health and revive their appetites. All the prisoners were sent home as soon as possible and they needed a prolonged convalescence. Later it was said that the Japanese ex-prisoners were never quite the same again and that their lives were blighted by their appalling ordeal. By comparison the fighting men had had an easier time of it.

While we were in Singapore the formal surrender of all Japanese forces in South-East Asia took place. By our ignominious defeats in Malaya and Singapore in 1942 the British had lost face throughout Asia. 'Face' is very important to Asians and we had lost it in a big way and would never again be seen as the imperial masters of empire. It was for this reason that Earl Mountbatten, the Supreme Allied Commander in South-East Asia, decided to humiliate the Japanese Signatories of the Peace Treaty, the senior Generals and Admirals assembled in Singapore, and make them lose face.

Officers and ratings from the fleet were allowed to witness the ceremony leading up to the signing of the surrender documents, which took place inside the Government Secretariat, an imposing white colonial building that was approached by a wide flight of steps. The Japanese Generals and Admirals were delivered in the back of army lorries and bundled out on to the pavement at the foot of the steps. They looked so small and insignificant beside their escorts and yet they had struck terror into so many of our soldiers, sailors and airmen. Each of these men was escorted by one guard drawn from the lowest ranking serviceman of each of the victorious nations, able seaman, private soldier or aircraftman, British, Australian, Indian or New Zealander. They were marched slowly up the long flight of steps at the top of which Admiral Mountbatten, General Slim and the Air Chief Marshal and other senior officers awaited them. As they reached the top of the steps Mountbatten and all the senior officers turned their backs on them and preceded them into the building. The ceremony was intended to degrade the enemy senior officers in front of the Singaporean crowd and it was extremely effective. There was complete silence as the Japanese walked up the steps and into the building, then an excited buzz of conversation broke out. It was a brilliant piece of theatre. After the ceremony the Japanese were pushed back up in to the backs of the lorries and driven away to imprisonment and, in some cases, to be tried and sentenced by the War Crimes Tribunal to death by hanging.

Although I understood the reason for this drama it really was the victors taking their revenge as they have done down the ages. Didn't the Romans parade defeated leaders through Rome before they were slaughtered, haltered and tied to wagons?

Soon after our stay in Singapore we got the glad news that we were to return home. The government was remarkably speedy in getting everyone back to the UK. After World War I the government had been slow to demobilise the troops and there had been mutinies by discontented soldiers. With a number of other ships of the Eastern Fleet we sailed back across the vast Indian Ocean rather slowly as we now had to economise in fuel. All through the war we had got used to speeding along at twenty knots to avoid submarine attack but now we were down to only fourteen knots. Once more we went through the Suez Canal and on to Malta to refuel and spend a couple of days to take on stores.

We had done our best to celebrate the end of the war in every port on our way home, Colombo, Aden, and Port Said, but Malta was special to sailors. So on our first night in Malta, our first in real civilisation, some of us decided to have a merry evening ashore, a good dinner and some fine wine and back to the ship by the last boat, which went at midnight. We were off to Gibraltar at the crack of dawn. We left it rather late to walk back the mile or so to the boat jetty and decided to hire a *gharri*. A *gharri* is a horse-drawn jalopy – one horse, one driver and two, or at a pinch, three passengers. We were four and we all squeezed in as the *gharri* sank on its springs. The driver was not too keen to take this boozy, overloaded crew, in more senses than one, back to Sliema. We exhorted him and his horse rather noisily and eventually we set forth.

After this somewhat hesitant start I decided we were too much of a load for the ancient gee gee and that it needed encouragement. So I disembarked and ran alongside the animal talking appropriate horsey language to it. This had a magical effect and the horse took off at speed. My friends, lounging in the passenger seat, egged it on. Thinking I had done my bit I tried to re-embark, but my dear friends fended me off. 'Keep going,' they cried. 'Keep at it; keep going.' Like hell I thought. I would show them and, flushed with wine, I ran the remaining mile to the jetty alongside the briskly trotting animal. By the time we arrived I was stone cold sober and virtue was rewarded.

We had a lot of harmless fun in *Tartar*. It was a happy and stimulating wardroom and it was sad to say goodbye to many delightful and interesting shipmates after we arrived in our home port at Plymouth. Once more I enjoyed that special sense of the sailor returning from the sea; once more that wonderful entrance to Plymouth Sound with the Cornish cliffs to port and the Devon coast to starboard and on the northern horizon the bold tors of Dartmoor beckoning me. And at last we were at peace. It was a supreme moment.

Chapter Eighteen

Rejoicing

Peace, Family and Home

O ur families were there to welcome us home. My mother and my other sailor brother came on board. Michael had been flown home from the Pacific as university students had priority for early demobilisation so that they could catch the autumn term at university. He had had a remarkable escape when two kamikaze aircraft hit his ship, HMS *Victorious*, on a suicide attack but he was unscathed. The ship was much damaged but survived. So our family suffered no wartime casualties.

In December I received a small bonus, a second 'mention in despatches', the absolute bottom of the class in the medals league, 'for services in the Far East'. God knows what they were, but I was not going to turn down a little gift like that.

Six years of war – six wasted years of my youth. Yet it had been an extraordinary experience. I had witnessed amazing acts of courage. Men and women found resources in themselves they didn't know they had and some apparently very ordinary people had achieved extraordinary things. We had had to take on exceptional responsibilities and had relished them with enthusiasm. For those who had survived the war had been transforming and exciting. Occasional moments of naked terror laid every quivering nerve bare, but were soon forgotten in an ecstasy of relief. Fear was a salutary whip to lash one to greater efficiency.

In all my jobs I felt a sense of achievement doing work that stretched me to the uttermost. I had survived unharmed and could look back at a fantastic experience, but not those who died. They were cut off in their prime. They had no life.

I finished my time in *Tartar* in a dry dock as a duty ship's officer doing fire duty, a sad end for a gallant fighting destroyer, also for me. It didn't last long and I soon found myself in a dank ex-nudist camp in a wood outside Plymouth, as the senior instructor at the Devonport Naval Signal School. The glory days were truly over, thank goodness, but it was a little sad.

Then it was home for my first peacetime Christmas in six years. This gave me pause to reflect on those lost war years. I could say the war had transformed me. From being a shy, diffident young man, uncertain of his naval career, I now knew I had the ability to tackle any job. I had learnt that I could face fear and disaster and that I would not be overcome. There might be upsets and sadness in my life but I would cope. I was ready for a new life.

That was how I felt as I arrived home for my leave. Any tendency to 'big-headedness' was rapidly knocked out of me by my family (brothers, cousins and mother) and the settled life of a Dartmoor village. 'It's been a terrible year for the potato crop and the sheep have....' 'Oh dear.' That puts one's own experiences into perspective.

Appendix

Memories from June 1940 for Remembrance Day 2005

S he rolled slowly over and sank gracefully beneath the waves. My home, my ship – not a great ship, just a little minesweeper, HMS *Skipjack*, who had cleared mines up and down the length of the Scottish and English coasts since the outbreak of war. Now she was a coffin for 294 soldiers rescued from the Dunkirk beaches and for nineteen of my shipmates.

Only a few minutes ago she had been fighting off an attack by dive-bombers. We were full of exhausted soldiers and were just starting home for Dover when out of a clear blue sky ten *Stukas* swooped down like buzzards on their prey. As navigator I was on the bridge conning the ship and I watched aghast as the bomb doors opened and what looked like large, black lozenges squirted out and tumbled towards us. The *Stukas* came so close I could see the pilots' faces framed in their black goggle helmets. Then an enormous crunch amidships. One bomb had ripped into the port oil fuel tank and another tore into the deck amidships. The rest missed. A great rent stretched across the midships deck from side to side. *Skipjack*'s back was broken. She was doomed.

There was nothing we could do. We were immobilised – no power, no engines, no steerage. Not to worry, we were soon put out of our misery. The same dive-bombers, circling overhead, screeched down again and the black lozenges spewed out. I almost waved to the pilots they were so close. One bomb seemed to be coming straight for the pit of my stomach. It nearly was. It hit the bridge ten feet away but did not explode. Three decks down it plunged and then there was a huge bang. A second bomb hit the forward gun position just below the bridge and a third ripped into the engine room.

There was a roar of explosions and a groan of buckling steel as the ship heeled over for her final plunge. The bridge became enveloped in acrid, black smoke and tongues of flame licked the burning paintwork. I seemed to be all alone. Were the others dead?

Unharmed, I struggled clear of the fire and smoke and jumped down to the deck below. By this time the ship had rolled over so far that the normally vertical ship's side was now a gentle slope into the sea, down which men were walking calmly and carefully. I joined them and swam away as far as I could to avoid the down suction as the ship sank.

It was a lovely day for a bathe. There was hot June sunshine and a sandy beach a few hundred yards away, but the enemy continued his attack on the survivors in the water and turned it into a nightmare. The sea was swarming with swimmers. We were not the only sunken ship that morning. Soldiers were crying 'Help' as they had no lifejackets. We all tried to help each other but it was a scene of chaos and many drowned.

My first feeling had been one of exhilaration. I had survived the sinking. I was fine. I was excited. There was no time to worry. Then fear kicked in as the falling bombs and machine-gunning continued and the oil fuel from burst ships' tanks coated the sea. We, the Dunkirk rescuers, became the rescued as we were eventually hauled out of the water and taken to Ramsgate.

Each year on Remembrance Day I grieve particularly for the 294 soldiers who thought they were safely on their way home and I also remember the nineteen individuals of our Ship's Company who gave their lives that day.

'Remember them'

Index